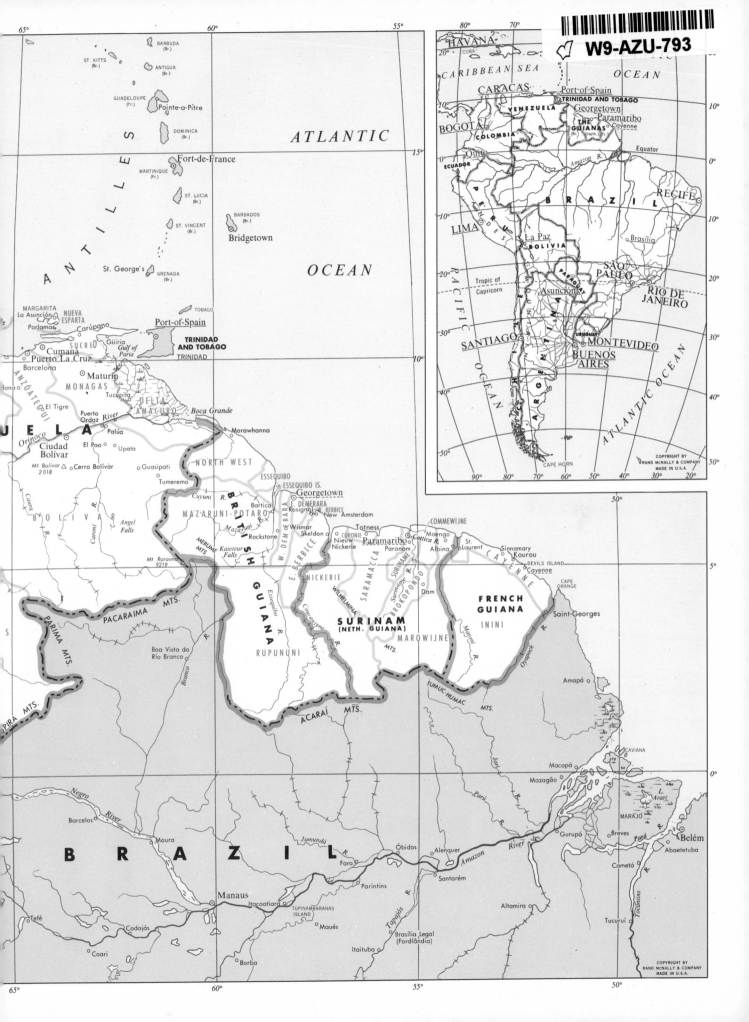

LIFE WORLD LIBRARY

COLOMBIA AND VENEZUELA

AND THE GUIANAS

TIME LIFE BOOKS

LIFE World Library

LIFE Nature Library

LIFE Science Library

The LIFE History of the United States

Great Ages of Man

LIFE Pictorial Atlas of the World

The Epic of Man

The Wonders of Life on Earth

The World We Live In

The World's Great Religions

The LIFE Book of Christmas

LIFE's Picture History of Western Man

The LIFE Treasury of American Folklore

America's Arts and Skills

300 Years of American Painting

The Second World War

LIFE's Picture History of World War II

Picture Cook Book

LIFE Guide to Paris

TIME Reading Program

LIFE WORLD LIBRARY

COLOMBIA AND VENEZUELA
AND THE GUIANAS

by Gary MacEoin

and The Editors of LIFE

TIME INCORPORATED   NEW YORK

COVER: Workmen spread coffee
beans drying in the sun
in the southern Colombian village
of San Agustín. Colombia's
high-quality coffee is the base
of the nation's economy.

ABOUT THE WRITER

Gary MacEoin, an Irish-born journalist and lawyer, went to the Caribbean area to edit a newspaper in 1944 and has been continuously involved in Latin American affairs ever since. He edited the Spanish-language monthly *La Hacienda* in New York for 12 years and has been the Caribbean and Latin American correspondent for a number of news agencies and publications. He has traveled throughout the continent to gather material for articles and books. Since 1961 he has written a weekly program for transmission in Latin America over the Voice of America. A 1962 book, *Latin America: The Eleventh Hour*, has been translated into French, German, Spanish and Italian. A longtime student of Spanish language, life and literature, Mr. MacEoin holds a Ph.D. degree from the National University of Ireland in his native Dublin and has written an interpretive biography of the great Spanish novelist Cervantes. Now a citizen of the United States with a home in New Jersey, Mr. MacEoin revisited Colombia, Venezuela and the Guianas while preparing this volume.

Contents

TIME-LIFE BOOKS

EDITOR
Norman P. Ross
EXECUTIVE EDITOR
Maitland A. Edey
TEXT DIRECTOR   ART DIRECTOR
Jerry Korn   Edward A. Hamilton
CHIEF OF RESEARCH
Beatrice T. Dobie
Assistant Art Director: Arnold C. Holeywell
Assistant Chief of Research: Monica O. Horne

•

PUBLISHER
Rhett Austell
General Manager: Joseph C. Hazen Jr.
Business Manager: John D. McSweeney
Circulation Manager: Joan D. Manley

LIFE MAGAZINE

EDITOR: Edward K. Thompson
MANAGING EDITOR: George P. Hunt
PUBLISHER: Jerome S. Hardy

LIFE WORLD LIBRARY

SERIES EDITOR: Oliver E. Allen
Editorial Staff for *Colombia and Venezuela and the Guianas:*
Assistant Editor: David S. Thomson
Designer: Ben Schultz
Chief Researcher: Grace Brynolson
Researchers: Jill Adams, Lea Guyer, Evelyn Hauptman,
Donald Newton, Louise Samuels, Ellen Youngblood

EDITORIAL PRODUCTION
Color Director: Robert L. Young
Copy Staff: Marian Gordon Goldman, Patricia Miller,
Dolores A. Littles
Picture Bureau: Margaret K. Goldsmith, Barbara Sullivan
Art Assistants: Douglas B. Graham, John M. Woods

The text for the chapters of this book was written by Gary MacEoin;
the picture essays were written by Frederick K. Poole. Many of the
photographs were taken by Arthur Rickerby. Valuable help was provided by the following individuals and departments of Time Inc.:
George Silk, Dmitri Kessel, LIFE staff photographers; Doris O'Neil,
Chief, LIFE Picture Library; Content Peckham, Chief, Bureau of Editorial
Reference; Richard M. Clurman, Chief, TIME-LIFE News Service; Mer-
cedez Vélez, Sandra Streepey and Alberto Cellario of LIFE EN ESPAÑOL.

Introduction

When Simón Bolívar, the Liberator, created Gran Colombia in 1821 after making most of the area independent of Spain, he dreamed of a geographical unit that would have fairly representative government and would set an example for the rest of the hemisphere. However, after eight years of existence Gran Colombia broke up into the countries of Colombia, Venezuela and Ecuador. Bolívar, in despair, later was to write that "those who have served the revolution have plowed the sea. We have tried all systems; nothing has proved effective."

The two largest nations, Colombia and Venezuela, went separate political ways, and it was not until a few years ago that their paths merged. In 1958 Dr. Alberto Lleras Camargo became Colombia's President after the overthrow of a military dictator, and in 1959 Rómulo Betancourt assumed power as the freely elected President of Venezuela. Betancourt was eventually to finish his five-year term of office, and for the first time in history a Venezuelan President was able to see his successor chosen in free elections. How fortunate were these countries to have statesmen of their caliber on the scene at these crucial moments in their history.

In this volume of the LIFE World Library series Gary MacEoin tells how Colombia, Venezuela and the Guianas by diverse paths reached their place in present-day history.

Colombia was governed by duly elected civilians of the dominant *criollo* group, the native-born white class that replaced the Spanish rulers, until a military strongman, General Gustavo Rojas Pinilla, took over in 1953. In Venezuela local strongmen, or *caudillos*, aided by their private armies, usually held sway until Antonio Guzmán Blanco and later Juan Vicente Gómez centralized their power toward the end of the 19th Century and established a national Army. In contrast to Venezuela the military stayed out of politics in Colombia and the Government seemed democratic, although the *criollos* really controlled the country. The colonial oligarchy was destroyed in Venezuela during the Federalist War (1858-1863), and in the years since that time there has been a most refreshing equality among the Venezuelans, no matter what their stations in life or the political system in effect. In Venezuela separation of state and Roman Catholic Church was pronounced; in Colombia the Church wielded great influence, especially in the field of education.

What lies ahead for these two countries?

Colombia has serious economic problems; banditry and Castro-Communist subversion are making maintenance of law and order difficult. With its oil riches Venezuela still remains the No. 1 target for violent take-over by Fidel Castro and his Communist allies. Nevertheless, the two countries appear to be securely in the fold of Latin American nations that have adopted representative democracy after a past history of civilian and military dictatorships.

Venezuela and Colombia have impressive records of social progress under the Alliance for Progress, especially in the fields of housing and education. Venezuela's agrarian-reform program is the best in the hemisphere. As a result of the cordial relations that have been established between themselves and the U.S. the two countries are seeking aid from the Alliance for Progress program for the joint economic development of a wide belt of rich land on either side of the border near the Andean cities of Cúcuta and San Cristóbal.

What satisfaction this state of affairs would give Simón Bolívar, who died believing his dream of strong, democratic nations in South America would never become a reality!

C. ALLAN STEWART
former U.S. Ambassador to Venezuela

People of Manizales, a city in the Colombian Andes, pause on a hilly street after a bullfight held in connection with their annual fair,

The Continent's Northern Tier

1

an event recently established to draw tourists. The austere mountain region is one of the fastest-growing areas in Colombia or Venezuela.

JUST below Panama's narrow neck, South America juts east a thousand miles on the 10th Parallel north latitude. A sailor following this sultry coastline seldom loses sight of the snow-capped Andes and their extension as the Segovia and Central Highlands of Venezuela. The mountains sweep east with the land, tree-clad to the water's edge. They end just in time to allow the Orinoco River to meander through its many outlets into the Atlantic. Far to the south, nearly 700 miles away, is the equator, paralleled almost all the way across the continent by the Amazon. In between are almost a million square miles of land, an area bigger than the United States from the Atlantic to the Mississippi.

Most of this vast area has proved so inhospitable that it has never been settled to any significant degree. The largest and least inviting of its regions is made up of plains, which the Spanish-speaking people call llanos. The great plains, parched and flooded by turn each year, form with the rain forests of the

Amazon three fifths of Colombia. They continue into Venezuela as the drainage basin of the Orinoco and occupy half its area. Almost equally forbidding are the Guiana Highlands, which rise between the plains and the Amazon, although this area has recently become a new frontier for Venezuelans eager to exploit its mountains of iron ore and to develop the vast hydroelectric potential of its waterfalls.

BECAUSE so much of the region is so inhospitable, the bulk of the people, some 25 million in all, live in mountain valleys in the three chains of the Andes which spread out over the west and north of Colombia and the north of Venezuela. Because the majority of the people live in valleys separated by Andean height, the area's population has tended to form isolated human islands. At the heart of each of these islands is a city. Until recently the cities were small, for the population was overwhelmingly rural, as was the economy. But no matter how small the city was, it dominated the surrounding area. Thus the early Spaniards planned it, developing both a systematic city plan and a rigid social structure to institutionalize their conquest. Their ideal was a tightly knit community, where all lived in the shadow of the cathedral and the town hall, where each knew his place and kept it. Only since the middle of the 20th Century has the system begun to sag under new stresses, an influx from the countryside swamping the city's facilities, an uprising of the docile workers challenging the monopoly of decision and power enjoyed from the beginning by the ruling classes.

The Spaniards, city people themselves, found it perfectly natural to impose a city culture on their new possessions. Early Spain had been similarly organized by overlords from the city-states of Greece, Carthage and Rome, and it had grown powerful in the Middle Ages as a series of kingdoms dominated by cities. For the Spaniards the city symbolized order, essential alike for the exercise of political control and the propagation of the Catholic religion.

As early as 1523, only 31 years after the first voyage of Columbus, the empire planners set forth in detail how to organize their New World cities. Each new city should have near it water, building materials, pasturelands and firewood. It should be at a moderate altitude, thus avoiding the transportation

problems of great heights and the health hazards of low-level swamps and lagoons. Fogbound places should be avoided. The rising sun should shine first on the town and not be reflected from a river into the eyes of the inhabitants. "Dirty and ill-smelling businesses" such as slaughterhouses and tanneries should be kept at a distance.

The plaza was planned as the hub of the city. Here were to be located the cathedral, the municipal buildings and the governor's palace. The size of the plaza would vary according to the size of the city, but it was always to be sufficiently spacious to permit displays of horsemanship. Bigger cities might have several minor neighborhood plazas.

The draftsmen worked their way out from the plaza. The streets were to run north and south, and east and west, at equal intervals, so that each block would be the same size. The leaders of the expedition founding the city were to be allotted the sites nearest the plaza, their stately mansions forming the upper-class quarter. Beyond them were to be located the service groups, the teachers, law clerks, civil servants, architects and storekeepers who would gradually form the nucleus of a middle class. Farther out were to be the workers' quarters.

THIS rigid if logical plan was followed over and over in all parts of Spanish America although today's visitor to Bogotá or Caracas, the capitals of Colombia and Venezuela, can scarcely reconstruct the original plan. Major arteries have been cut through the old centers to stimulate the flow of honking private cars and frenzied taxis. Blocks of patioed colonial homes have yielded to multistoried shops and offices. But elsewhere time has almost stood still. The weekly market in small Andean towns is still held in the ancient plaza where black-hatted Indian women and their squat menfolk form random groups. Trucks parked alongside the sturdy mules constitute the most noticeable concession to modernity, although the Indians' bright homespuns and graceful clay pots are fighting a losing battle in the market stalls with store clothing and aluminum ware.

What change there is began only recently, and it was largely spurred by the modern breakthroughs in transportation. Andean towns which from colonial times to the 1920s were difficult four- and five-day rides on muleback from Bogotá may now be only a few hours away by fast highway, an hour by airplane.

The big cities have grown rapidly bigger for the same reason, and because of increased industry and commerce. Caracas in 1930 had three times as many people as during the Wars of Independence (1810-1824), but its essential character remained. Life centered around the plaza. Somberly dressed descendants of generals and presidents walked from the great mansions to Sunday service in the nearby cathedral. Their sons and daughters strolled on the plaza's paths in the balmy late afternoon. The narrow valley still allowed a generous hinterland of sugar cane estates on its flat bottom lands and coffee farms on its slopes.

Since 1930, however, Caracas has trebled its population once more and burst in flood in all directions to the mountain barrier. The few estates that remain are less a source of income than the flaunting of a wealth that can afford its private park in the shadow of skyscrapers. Nor can they long survive the tunnels, viaducts, highways, supermarkets, baseball stadiums and playgrounds which multiply around them. Gone is the prim checkerboard of adobe-walled low buildings, blank to the street but bright with flowers and dripping water in the interior sun-drenched patios. Expansion follows no detectable order or design, now dense, now scattered, the present jostling the past. Here the skyscraper has achieved distinctive qualities with a wide variety of forms, materials, textures and spatial relationships. Colorful murals, tiles and mosaics enliven the faces of the buildings. The effect is dazzling: the viewer, sated with brightness, sees the buildings vibrate against the purple splendor of the encircling hills.

CARACAS has grown, but the bustling crowd on the sidewalks continues to show the same fascinating variety as before. The soldier in olive drab has the pudgy round face of the Indian from the mountains near the Colombian border. The white-collared priest has the same lean, angular jaw as the Spaniards of the Basque country. The rotund shopkeeper is Syrian and the tight-sheathed, fashionable señorita has the high cheekbones and slanted eyes of China. The porter pushing the handcart is a Negro. And the ubiquitous children reflect the kaleidoscopic permutations of centuries of people living together. The language has words to describe the major kinds of crossbreeding—*mulato* (Negro and white), *zambo* (Negro and Indian), *pardo* (white, Indian and Negro). Most important of all is *mestizo*, originally meaning a white-Indian combination but today broadened to describe the man of tomorrow, the race that is emerging as a synthesis of many races.

The mingling of the races dates from the first European settlements. The leaders of the expeditions in their exclusive homes adjoining the town plazas and in their subsequently built country mansions stressed their European origins. They sent to Spain for their wives and boasted of their "white blood." But they often had children by Indian women and they often acknowledged them. Quite illogically, they insisted on calling them white. It was a significant trait. Logic never counted for much with these hard-headed individualists. If they said the child was white, it was white.

THE Spanish Crown carried the process a step farther. Successful *pardos* who were members of the artisan class could buy a document which proclaimed them and their families "white." The effect was to make them members of the upper class with all the accompanying privileges. These letters of patent issued by the Crown were bitterly resented by the Creoles, the people of wholly Spanish origins born in America. To allow people of mixed racial background to enter their class and in effect to become Creoles, too, diluted their privileged status. But the Crown continued to exercise its prerogative. It was not only a question of revenue. The authorities in Madrid were in constant conflict with the Creoles. They distrusted anyone not born in Spain. In fact, they reserved all top posts for the Spanish-born, *peninsulares* as they called them.

The Creoles described the *peninsulares* more expressively. They were *gachupines*, the "spurred ones" who rode roughshod over all others, or *godos*, a Spanish word for the barbarian Visigoths who centuries earlier had conquered Spain. Even today, Colombia's reactionaries are called *godos*.

Below the "whites" came the mestizos. The rank-and-file of the Spaniards took Indian wives, and their offspring became the workers in the towns and the peasant farmers and farm laborers in the country. At first, the main rural labor force was pure Indian, living at a lower social and economic level than the mestizos. The consistent policy of Spain, however, was to assimilate the Indians into the mestizo class, an objective achieved in part by miscegenation, in part by the imposition of religion, language, dress and other culture traits. When Negro labor was imported, it formed a separate class below that of the mestizos. A process of assimilation began almost immediately and was completed by the abolition of slavery. From that time on, all Negroes have formed part of the mestizo class, although they have tended to be regarded as the lower element in it.

The Indians in the settled areas around the cities have long since been fully incorporated into the same class. In a few places, particularly in the southern highlands of Colombia, some groups of Indians have survived on communal landholdings granted them by the Spanish Crown in the early 17th Century. They have adopted many elements of Spanish culture and most speak Spanish, but their customs clearly distinguish them from the mestizos and they retain a consciousness of themselves as Indians. Elsewhere, in the llanos and tropical forests, some tribes continue to live in primitive conditions, each with a distinct language and way of life. Estimates of numbers are vague and conflicting. Unassimilated Indians in Venezuela may total 90,000; in Colombia, perhaps three times that number.

WHEN the vast majority of the inhabitants lived on the land, as was true well into the 20th Century, there was almost no opportunity for the mestizo or Indian to rise in the social scale. He was a virtual serf, and there was no intermediate step between him and the big estate owner on whom he absolutely depended. With the growth of the cities, however, and the expansion of trade and commerce in the 19th Century, the middle class began to grow and to absorb members from the top of the mestizo class. This expansion was much less rapid than that of the middle classes in North America and Western Europe, and the middle class in Colombia and Venezuela was much less successful in its efforts to win recognition as a social force. But during the present century the middle class has become more assertive.

Growth of industry has added to its numbers and has provided an ally in organized labor. These two groups have provided the major impetus for the spread of education, including expansion of the universities, and they have in turn utilized the university students as a political force to further their interests. The growth of this class is more advanced in Venezuela, whose huge oil industry has replaced the traditional estate agriculture as the basis of the economy. Since 1958, Venezuela has been ruled by governments reflecting primarily the views of the middle class. But even in Venezuela the final arbiter is still the Army, an element from the old power structure.

THE middle class is not alone in having become more assertive; so have the workers, and they have created considerable social unrest by calling for a further redistribution of power in the society in both countries. This lower class is not only changing its attitudes and functions but is splitting into two parts. The process began in the 1930s when improved public health and sanitation and the elimination of malaria and other endemic diseases started a steep rise in the rural population. The absence of outlets for the growing labor force in both countries prompted massive movements of unskilled workers to the cities—whose economies were unable to absorb most of them. The newcomers have squatted wherever they could find unoccupied land, have built themselves shacks and proceeded to raise families. Some cities, like Bogotá, manage to keep these newcomers discreetly hidden. In others, like Caracas, they are as evident on the hillsides as the vultures who compete with them for scraps and garbage.

Illiterate, undernourished and unskilled, these new nomads make no contribution to the productive capacity of their countries. Statisticians and politicians are beginning to call them unemployables, because they lack the training to work even if work were available. The birth rate of these "unemployables" is substantially higher than that of their fellow citizens and each year they become a heavier albatross hanging around the neck of the productive economy. It is this mass that constitutes the greatest factor of social unrest and the greatest threat to democracy in both Colombia and Venezuela. Unless

COLOMBIA

TWO SIMILAR FLAGS WITH HISTORIC ORIGINS

The flags of Colombia and Venezuela have stripes of the same colors—*(from the top)* yellow, blue and red—that marked the flag carried by the victorious armies of Simón Bolívar. Colombia's flag is the same as Bolívar's, with a broad top stripe of yellow. The Venezuelan flag was altered to add stars representing the seven Venezuelan provinces that originally revolted from Spain.

VENEZUELA

economic development can be speeded up fast enough to assimilate it, the future holds little hope.

Since World War II, the explosion of communications—newspapers and periodicals, movies, radio and television—has made an impact everywhere. The jukebox, the soda fountain and other cultural traits of the United States are in evidence even in remote villages, and in the cities one might easily be deceived into thinking that the old ways are dead.

The reality is more complicated. The traditions of 400 years do not disappear in one generation. The upper class has no intention of abdicating its privileges. Aristocratic parents still train their sons to carry themselves with dignity and reserve, and remind them that they are the descendants or relatives of presidents, generals, archbishops, poets and heroes. The family leaders point to their names in the history books. They glory in the coats of arms emblazoned over their front doors as evidence of their pre-eminence in the community.

A sentimental attachment to the past is not the only motivation of the upper class. Its members enjoy modern living. The luxury of their homes and clubs is seldom matched in the United States, and behind their closed doors they share with their friends the kind of life they have learned to enjoy on their long visits abroad. But they resist the social leveling that is an integral part of this international culture. Their most treasured value is their status as a ruling class. The formalities which they observe and impose in public constitute the daily recognition and expression of their importance. These they will not yield without a struggle.

The middle class, meanwhile, is trapped in a vicious economic cycle. To move upward means to acquire the qualities and status symbols of the upper class. Sons must be put through school, and at least

one through a university. Clothes must be bought and appearances kept up. But as the need for money increases, the ways in which it can be made grow more limited. The old Spanish aristocratic feeling persists that no man who works with his hands, or even works very hard, can be a gentleman. Accordingly, even if the father is the owner of a store, the menial source of the family income must be soft-pedaled. To maintain a front of prosperity, the family will go short of food and house furnishings. Between concern for appearances and struggling to make ends meet, there is little time to enjoy life.

TO those accustomed to the casual living characteristic of the United States, all of this appears a very straight and narrow path. Such it is in fact for unmarried girls and young matrons of the upper and middle classes. Once girls reach their teens their freedom of action is progressively restricted. Their mothers, aunts and older sisters watch their comings and goings. Boisterous activities are discouraged and the ladylike graces are inculcated. Companions and boyfriends are screened. Dating is becoming more common in big cities, especially among university coeds, but many families still frown on the practice, and the social life of the adolescent girl is largely limited to home and school and to well-chaperoned encounters and parties.

Nevertheless, the mold is cracking. Women with higher education tend to be less concerned with such conventions, and opt for emancipation. The woman who participates and excels in politics, sports, business, a profession or the arts is no longer an oddity, but neither is she very common.

The standards for men have always been quite different. Publicly and officially, they are expected to maintain the same well-mannered decorum as their

13

womenfolk. But they are also expected to be asser- tive, to play the role of the ardent male. Since they cannot strut and boast of conquests within their own class, where the women are supposed to be sacrosanct, the socially approved solution is to frequent the red-light district, which is a discreet but important feature of the typical city. Public reaction to such activities and to extramarital affairs is more indulgent than it is in the United States, and most upper-class husbands at one time or another unobtrusively maintain a mistress.

Social toleration of conduct directly at odds with the moral teachings of the faith professed by most Colombians and Venezuelans suggests that religion does not mean quite the same thing for them as for the average North American. The Latin American sees religion more as a way of life than as a code of conduct. If challenged, he will agree that he is not living up to his obligations, but in practice the impulse or desire of the moment weighs more heav- ily than theoretical considerations of right and wrong. Nor is his ambivalence restricted to ethics and moral conduct. In politics, he can take a position of ex- treme opposition to the Roman Catholic Church as an institution without regarding himself or being regarded by his friends as having ceased to be a member of the Church in good standing.

THIS apparently contradictory behavior flows from a concept of the individual quite differ- ent from that held by the average North American or North European. Anarchism as a philosophy has al- ways had such a deep appeal for Spaniards that many Spanish political theorists justify their country's present authoritarian government as being essential to prevent national disintegration. The Latin Amer- ican honors his Spanish heritage by offering a con- stant challenge to the state, to society and to every other man. He makes his decision and rejects the right of any power on earth to challenge it. In the words of a 17th Century bishop of Caracas: "My jurisdiction extends as far as I want it to."

Such attitudes underlie many aspects of Colom- bian and Venezuelan life that make little sense to the outsider. They are ultimately disruptive of soci- ety, equally removed from Rousseau's theory that mankind has voluntarily undertaken to accept the

decisions of the majority—the Social Contract—and from the pragmatic compromise which inspires pol- itics, business and human relations in the United States. The effects are particularly evident in pol- itics. A brilliant and patriotic band of Venezuelans joined Rómulo Betancourt in the late 1930s to form the nation's first truly democratic party, and they supported this party during its brief period of power from 1945 to 1948. But by the end of Betan- court's second term as President in 1963 they were splintered into five warring factions. Issues between them were far less substantial than are those be- tween the progressive and conservative wings of either of the major United States parties. But neither the experience of a destructive dictatorship between 1948 and 1958 nor the continuing threat of a new dictatorship could persuade them to sink their triv- ial differences.

GLORIFICATION of individuality does not make for easy living. What strikes the visitor from the United States is the air of formality. As an antidote to the usual stiffly formal behavior, a more friendly ritual called the *abrazo*, or embrace, proves useful. The bigger the audience, the more effusive the greeting. Two soberly dressed men will sudden- ly spring from armchairs on opposite sides of a hotel lobby and trot toward each other with little inarticu- late cries of pleasure, throw their arms around each other and pat their mutual backs to exhaustion.

The direct negative comes easy in business in the United States, but in Colombia and Venezuela it is unspeakably discourteous. It is better to ignore an- other's presence than deny his request. The countless favor-seekers sitting in the reception rooms of count- less offices are never told that the managing director is too busy to see them. The bouffant-haired secre- tary is adept at simply not noticing their presence. If one of them insists on being recognized, she tells him to wait, or to come back tomorrow at 10 o'clock. If one of these supplicants does succeed in waylay- ing the managing director, he is told that yes, his re- quest is being considered and that yes, there should be a decision tomorrow. From such inconclusive an- swers the favor-seeker is expected to read the signs, for the rule is well known that 10 yeses make a no. Even if the answer is going to be yes, the approach remains important. Nothing irritates the Latin American more than the salesman who charges in with a business deal all wrapped up, the documents sworn, the checks certified. For the Latin American, people are more important than papers. It is the relationship of trust with other men that counts. Business, like marriage, should be preceded by a graceful courtship.

An emphasis on the individual's sacred commitment to follow his own instinct without permitting appeal to an outside court of reason is deep in the soil of Spain. Cervantes described it when he made Don Quixote say of the lady whom he imagined he loved, "God knows whether or not there is a Dulcinea in this world. . . . I contemplate her *as she needs must be.*"

Conditions in the New World ensured the deepening of attitudes inherited from Spain. A man needed supreme confidence to ford rivers, climb over mountains, survive diseases, fight Indians. His isolation in his city was complete. Up to 1930, it was as easy to go from Popayán in southwestern Colombia to San Francisco, California, as to Bogotá.

Such isolation from each other and from the center of political authority caused each of the cities hidden in the folds of the Andes to become a law and a nation unto itself. The cities did not challenge the king's authority. They welcomed his messenger, then stored the decrees away and ignored them. They fought frequently among themselves before, during and after the Wars of Independence. They developed strong regional loyalties and distinctive characteristics.

SOME cities ascribe their real or imagined virtues to their special racial composition. This is particularly true of the people of the Antioquia region, whose center is Medellín, where the settlers were mainly from the Basque provinces and from the Spanish region of Asturias. Many Negroes were imported to Antioquia, and a recent observer has described the result as "a pious, proud and prosperous mestizo-Mulatto people, [the] self-styled Yankees of South America." Others compare them to Texans for their exaggerations. Today they are found as business leaders all over Colombia.

Other Colombians make the singsong accent of the *Antioqueño* the butt of friendly jesting, and Venezuelans similarly make fun of the speech patterns of *Maracuchos,* natives of Maracaibo. The *Maracucho* takes it in his stride. Such is his regional pride that one is reputed to have commented atop the Eiffel Tower: "If only Paris had a lake like ours, it would look like Maracaibo."

So it goes from city to city. Old Caracas had a bar on every corner; mile-high Mérida has a church on every street. Bogotá has a sobriety to match the gray skies of its high plateau. It distrusts sunshine, preferring the familiar overcast, and Bogotá newspapers note that sunny days mean cold nights and a water shortage. The Cali people are industrious, intelligent and imaginative. But in Cartagena on the Caribbean, one is on a different planet. The city is fun-loving and relaxed, a perfect setting for the African music of its Negro citizens. The steaming humidity inhibits exertion. Men mummified by salt spray and tropic sun doze in the chairs of innumerable barbers.

THE city as an institution has played a smaller part in the history of the region east of Venezuela known as the Guianas, a major part of which came under the political control of The Netherlands, France and England. The only settlements for about two centuries after its discovery were transient camps to serve traders, smugglers and pirates. Even sovereignty was long in dispute. The Spaniards regarded the other claimants as trespassers but made little effort to eject them. The coastal climate was unhealthy and the forest of the interior impenetrable. The vast extent of the more attractive lands controlled by the Spaniards engaged their full efforts.

The English, French and Dutch had much more trouble from one another. The Dutch were the original settlers of British Guiana, and the English founded Dutch Guiana (now Surinam) and Paramaribo, its capital. The English seized the Dutch settlements in 1665, but soon gave them back and also relinquished Paramaribo in exchange for New York. A century later, the English ousted the Dutch from their holdings, only to be ejected in turn by the French. In 1803 the English again occupied all three Guianas and held them until the Congress of Vienna in 1815 established the division that has since persisted.

A coastal strip usually 15 to 20 miles wide has constituted the principal exploited resource of the Guianas ever since the first European settlements. Vast quantities of silt carried by the Amazon far out to sea, discoloring the ocean for 200 miles offshore, are swept by currents along the coast to form rich alluvial deposits at or near high-tide level. The Dutch were familiar with the drainage of low coasts and they undertook the first of the engineering works which protect much of British Guiana and Surinam behind sea walls and permit farming of the alluvial soils.

The population of the three Guianas has always been concentrated on these coastal strips. Inland, past mangrove swamps, the forest begins, trackless, endless. Here Indians live much as they lived before the white men came, nomadic, building small family villages near creeks and rivers, and moving when food is scarce. Cassava, the grated manioc root, is their staple food. Proteins come from monkey stew seasoned with herbs and spices, and from snakes, worms, insects, currants, nuts and palm cabbage.

Also in the forest, and at a level only slightly less primitive than that of the Indians, live the Bush Negroes, or, as they prefer to be called, the Bush people. These descendants of runaway slaves are found mostly in Surinam, where they constitute 11 per cent of the population. Many of the Bush people like to live near waterfalls or on island clusters in a cataract complex, a practice probably developed as a protection against slave raiders. Skilled boatbuilders and boatmen, they work for mining, timber and agricultural enterprises.

THE early European settlers tried to make the Indians serve as a labor force. In this they were no more successful than were the Spaniards on the West Indian islands and in the coastal areas of the Caribbean. Soon they began to import Negro slaves and develop an economy based on tobacco and sugar. The abolition of slavery in the mid-19th Century sent the planters scurrying in all directions. White workers were brought from many European countries but they soon died off. Only Portuguese Jews who had fled persecution in Brazil survived, and even they quickly moved from agriculture to the towns. Asiatic Indians proved the most adaptable. Today they are the main source of agricultural labor in British Guiana and Surinam, supplemented by Javanese in Surinam. In French Guiana, plantation agriculture has decayed.

Bad living conditions and endemic diseases kept the Guianas perennially short of workers until the 1920s when medical advances began to curb malaria and other tropical scourges. Since that time, just as in Colombia and Venezuela, the population has been growing faster than the economy, producing similar social stresses. The pressure has been eased slightly in Surinam and British Guiana by the development of bauxite mining and the growth of small industries.

THE class structure of society has always been even more pronounced in the Guianas than in Colombia and Venezuela. Political control was exercised from the European capital of the colonizing power until after World War II, the interests of the small white management group always being given priority. This group, for its part, identified itself with the colonizing power and insisted on racial purity for membership. Much miscegenation occurred, especially with the Negroes in the early period, but the offspring were not admitted to white society and simply became the upper stratum of the Negro group. Nor were the Portuguese admitted to full membership in the upper class. They follow immediately after it as a subdivision of the middle class to which many Negroes and some Asiatic Indians have gained entry during the present century.

The racial character of the class structure remains important in British Guiana, where British capital still controls the major industries, and there is considerable animosity between the Negroes and the East Indians. In French Guiana, on the contrary, the process of blending the races into a single mestizo class like that of Colombia and Venezuela is much farther advanced. Surinam occupies an intermediate position. The principal racial groups retain their distinct cultures, languages and sense of group identity, especially in the rural areas. Their political allegiance is also racially conditioned. But the political leaders of the various races work together in harmonious coalition. In addition, intermarriage is becoming more common in the cities. Even the Chinese shopkeepers who long kept aloof are now marrying people of other racial backgrounds. It would seem that in this small corner of the world, love and the mobile capitalistic society have cooperated to produce a bright example of racial harmony.

Mid-afternoon idlers gather around an ornate Spanish lamppost in Cartagena, an old Colombian port city with fortresslike walls.

The Surprising Prevalence of Flourishing Cities

The cities of Colombia, Venezuela and the Guianas are old and established—and growing at a furious pace. The Spanish were great city builders and since their conquest the region has had a surprisingly urban flavor. Recently economic pressures have caused many of these cities to grow dramatically. Colombia's Bogotá and Venezuela's Caracas have more than doubled in size since 1950. Sometimes these cities appear more modern than New York, sometimes more Old World than Seville. But whatever their outward forms, to most of their inhabitants they hold a promise of progress and 20th Century comforts.

17

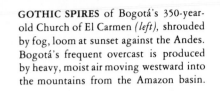

GOTHIC SPIRES of Bogotá's 350-year-old Church of El Carmen *(left)*, shrouded by fog, loom at sunset against the Andes. Bogotá's frequent overcast is produced by heavy, moist air moving westward into the mountains from the Amazon basin.

GRIM GARGOYLES atop an old Government building, and a church spire, contrast with the steel and glass headquarters of the Banco de la República *(opposite)*. Though isolated in the Andes, Bogotá became a major Spanish-American city.

COLOMBIA'S CAPITAL, *Bogotá is a mixture of old Spanish monuments and the most modern architecture*

HOTEL BALCONIES look down on the traffic and other new buildings in central Bogotá *(left)*. Because fog veils the sunlight, Bogotá's architecture is closer to that of North American cities than that of the sunnier sections of South America.

SATURDAY STROLLERS returning from a bullfight crowd the modern streets of downtown Bogotá *(above)*. Despite Bogotá's new buildings and roadways, its pace is leisurely, in keeping with *bogotanos'* feeling for their Old World heritage.

19

A FUTURISTIC AUDITORIUM by Venezuelan architect Carlos Raúl Villanueva houses Caracas' cultural events such as the jazz concert shown above in rehearsal.

BIG HOUSING PROJECTS, many of them built in the 1950s under dictator Pérez Jiménez, dominate Caracas (*right*) but fail to keep up with its rising population.

AN OLD STATUE honoring 19th Century poet Andrés Bello is overshadowed by a new building (*below*), as if symbolizing the triumph of modernity in Caracas.

urface affluence of a city that places modernity before tradition

A NEW EXPRESSWAY cutting through Caracas is one of many built by Pérez Jiménez in his program of using Venezuela's oil money to modernize the capital.

AN EXPENSIVE HOTEL, a failure of Pérez Jiménez's building program *(below)*, stands on a mountain above the city. Because of inaccessibility it has few guests.

FRENCH-STYLE CAFE in Cayenne, French Guiana *(above)*, has a distinctly languorous and tropical air despite its attempt to look Parisian. French Guiana is technically a Department of Metropolitan France and sends representatives to the French Congress, but it remains economically backward.

ENGLISH-LANGUAGE SIGNS adorn an office building *(left)* in Georgetown, capital of British Guiana, although some signs advertise businesses run by Asian Indians. Fierce rivalry between the colony's Indians and Negroes has caused political turmoil and postponed independence.

DUTCH-BUILT CITY of Paramaribo, Surinam's capital *(opposite)*, combines close-packed houses and an air of order, like a tropical parody of an old town in the Low Countries. The statue of Mahatma Gandhi *(foreground)* was erected by Indians. Paramaribo's harbor is in the background.

The Dream
of El Dorado

LIKE the discovery of writing, of the wheel, of gunpowder, of how to split the atom or of how to orbit spacecraft, the discovery of America belongs among the great moments of human history.

Europe was ready to open up some new lands. It was beginning to develop the know-how that would blossom into the Industrial Revolution. More goods were being manufactured and new markets were needed. The techniques of navigation were being improved. Agriculture lagged, however, and because so much of Europe was farmed inefficiently or not at all even the area's then small population seemed to need more living space. The hostile Turkish Empire blocked the logical routes of expansion by land to the south and east. Europeans needed some escape route westward. But they were no more prepared to deal with what they did find than are today's space explorers for the intelligent beings they may discover as unexpectedly as Columbus discovered South America's Indians.

The Europeans were not even sure that the Indians, as they insisted on miscalling them, were human beings. Did they have immortal souls? Should they be baptized? These were no idle questions. For Columbus and the powerful Spanish nation that he served, the spreading of the Christian gospel was as integral a part of national policy as are the preservation and expansion of democracy for the United States today. The theologians soon decided that the Indians did in fact have immortal souls and were proper subjects for conversion. Unfortunately for the Indians, they wore gold ornaments and pearls. The Spaniards had set out not only to spread the gospel but to trade in the spices of the East. The prospect of finding great wealth in gold and pearls softened their disappointing failure to find the spice routes. And the slight regard the Indians had for the ornaments they wore seemed to prove conclusively that the land was full of riches.

In the perspective of history the contradiction between the two aims of the explorers is obvious. One can only note that the Spaniards were not unique in their self-deception. The colonialism of the 19th Century was equally ambivalent. And even today many seek to link aid to developing nations with commercial profits.

A FURTHER complicating factor existed then as now. Today the East-West struggle colors every contact between the great powers and the small ones. Sixteenth Century Europe was locked in a north-south conflict in which the contenders considered the stakes as high as we regard those in the struggle between Communism and democracy. Spain was the bulwark and leader of the southern faction. The challengers were France and England. Soon they would be joined by Holland, as yet a part of the Holy Roman Empire and within Spain's sphere of influence, but shortly destined to win independence and play a major role in the exploration of new lands.

Spain did not always see eye to eye with Portugal, its principal partner. Portugal, first in the discovery business, wanted to keep all it had found. The two finally submitted their problem to the Pope, one of whose many functions was to serve as a kind of international court. A stroke of the papal quill divided the world with a north-south line finally placed 370 leagues west of the Cape Verde Islands. It gave the Portuguese a toe hold just south of the Guianas, where the South American continent juts east into the Atlantic, a toe hold that they gradually expanded to the present dimensions of Brazil.

Spain and Portugal both agreed to the Pope's division. But Europe's northern nations were not impressed with what the Pope had done. "The sun shines for me as well as for the others," was the scornful reaction of Francis I of France. "I should very much like to see the clause in Adam's will that excludes me from a share of the world." He had no scruple about preying on Spain's American preserves. Still less had England and Holland when the 16th Century Protestant Reformation introduced an additional factor of conflict between them and Roman Catholic Spain.

The Spaniards tried to hide their discoveries, as do the Russians their space probes. Rumors, nevertheless, drifted to Paris and London, provoking quick reactions of fear and cupidity. Columbus on his third voyage just escaped an intercepting French fleet. Others were less lucky. As evidence mounted that Spain's conquistadors had discovered fabulous wealth in South America, the English and French built bigger fleets to seize the Spanish convoys.

It was a vicious cycle. Spain needed more and more gold to maintain naval supremacy, while only part of what it extracted from South America got past the bold and watchful privateers. The Indians were the ones who got the worst of it. The theologians had declared them human and the lawyers had written them a substantial bill of rights. But what mattered in practice was that the Spanish adventurers were required to send vast stores of wealth back to the mother country, and they were their own judges of the methods they used to get them.

IN this climate of conflicting objectives the exploration of the new lands went forward. Amerigo Vespucci, like Columbus an Italian in Spain's service, in 1499 sailed south along the Brazilian coast and passed the mouth of the Amazon. Turning north, he skirted the Guiana coast, sailed past the mouth of the Orinoco and dropped anchor at Trinidad. He then went west along the Venezuelan coast and appears to have proceeded some miles beyond the Gulf of Venezuela before turning north once more for Hispaniola. In all he observed or explored some 3,000 miles of coastline.

Vespucci's companion, Alonso de Ojeda, or possibly Vespucci himself, entered Lake Maracaibo on the way. They called the area Venezuela, Spanish for "little Venice," because the lake dwellers built their huts on stilts and used waterways as streets. On this and later voyages Vespucci confirmed what Columbus had begun to suspect—that here was a hitherto unknown land and not, as they had hoped, a part of the fabled Indies. He proclaimed his discovery so widely that by 1507 the continent was beginning to be called Amerigo's Land on maps. The first finder, Columbus, did not have a single country named for him for more than three centuries.

From the Amazon to the Orinoco the coast offered mud, swamp, rain forest and disease. The Spaniards claimed it and ignored it, preferring the climate and prospects farther north. First to be settled, in 1520, were the islands of Cubagua and Margarita. A barren rock lacking even water and firewood, Cubagua possessed oyster beds rich in pearls. Here was built Nueva Cádiz, which soon had 1,000 inhabitants and was for 20 years the most prosperous town in these "West Indies."

ON the whole, nevertheless, the Caribbean area was not living up to the expectations and needs of the adventurers. A series of hurricanes and an earthquake in 1543 destroyed the oyster beds and it gradually became evident that the gold ornaments worn by the mainland Indians did not prove the presence of significant deposits. Either they represented the slow accumulation of many generations or had trickled to the coast from great distances inland. The latter supposition was confirmed by the testimony of the Indians themselves.

For a time the major Spanish expeditions bypassed Venezuela. Prospects of quick wealth seemed brighter in the north, where Hernán Cortés had overthrown the empire of the Aztecs, and in the southwest, where Francisco Pizarro and his brothers were conquering that of the Incas. But a few could not get the myth of El Dorado out of their heads and continued to believe that a city of gold would be found somewhere in the area covered by present-day Colombia and Venezuela.

The original legend of El Dorado concerned an Indian chief—"the gilded one"—who covered himself with gold dust for certain ceremonies, but eventually the phrase came to mean an immensely rich city or region. To find this realm of gold, adventurers probed along the coast and up the rivers, led expeditions into the interior and built bases from which to organize a systematic search of the hinterland. In their minds, gold and glory were always uppermost. They had not left Europe, as many North American colonists had, to escape war or persecution, nor did they propose to carve a homestead from virgin territory. But while seeking gold and glory they had to eat, and that meant that food had to be grown. Then, as the illusion of ready-made wealth faded, many cut their dreams down to size and adjusted to living off the land.

They still, nevertheless, refused to work with their hands, a trait that persists among Latin America's upper classes and has spread to the new middle class. Instead, they conveniently decided to make the Indians do the dirty work. The Indians found it less convenient. They lacked the physical stamina for steady exertion. In the gold mines on the island of Hispaniola, under Spanish overseers, they died off like flies. Bartolomé de Las Casas, the first monk to protest effectively against Spanish cruelty to the Indians, put the life expectancy of a pearl fisher in Cubagua at one year. To replace casualties the Spaniards raided the mainland, following the routes discovered by seekers of El Dorado.

THE explorers and raiders found many kinds of Indians. All had more or less the physical characteristics Columbus had noted when he laid eyes on them for the first time on October 12, 1492. They were "of the tanned color of Canary Islanders, neither black nor white." Their hair was black, "not kinky but straight and coarse like horsehair." Their foreheads were broad, their eyes handsome and not small, and their "legs very straight, all in a line; and no belly, but very well built."

The Indians proved to have varied standards of sexual morality, some tribes being puritanical in their customs, some monogamous, others polygamous, some given to wife swapping. The status of women also varied greatly. In some tribes the roles of the sexes, except the biological, were reversed, the women doing the hard labor and the men domestic tasks. In some the men and women spoke different languages. There was even said to be a tribe whose women used a language among themselves that was kept secret from the men. Early travelers commented frequently on the attractive women of the mainland. "Fair of feature . . . with more grace than other women of the new world," says one. "The prettiest and most lovable of any that I have seen in the Indies," reports another. But they were not to be trifled with. One Carib girl near Cartagena killed eight Spaniards of a landing party before she was overcome.

Indians originally arrived in the area between the Orinoco River and the Caribbean coast more than 10,000 years ago. For about 5,000 years they lived by hunting giant prehistoric animals, such as the mammoth and the mastodon, but as these species gradually became extinct, the Indians turned to gathering fruits, berries, roots and grubs. Those living on the coast also ate fish and shellfish. Then, about 1000 B.C., a number of groups of Indians began to develop primitive methods of agriculture. Among the most widespread of the Indian peoples who farmed were the Arawaks. The Arawaks were later driven from much of their territory by a migration of the more warlike Carib Indians.

The Caribs were notable navigators by river and sea. Canoes carrying 50 men were used to trade in clothing, drugs, salt, cotton, skins, rubber, cacao, gold and slaves. While less advanced than the Chibchas of the Colombian Andes, let alone the Incas or the Aztecs, some of these tribes had a primitive token system, using shell disks as money.

THE Spaniards found many Indians engaged in settled agriculture, as well as many nomads on the plains and savannas and along the rivers. None of them knew the wheel, nor did they use metal for tools or implements. The lowland Indians used the slash-and-burn method of farming. They felled trees and burned the undergrowth to create a clearing. Then they planted corn or tubers until soil exhaustion forced them to move and clear another section of forest. More sophisticated methods were used by Indians living on the Andean slopes, including terracing and irrigation. Some of the tribes kept bees for their honey. Many domesticated wild hogs, turkeys, ducks and other local fowl.

The primitive level of agriculture kept population density very low. Spanish slave raids cut the numbers further. Tribes that had welcomed the explorers fought the slavers. In addition, the slavers apparently encouraged one tribe to raid another and sell the captives.

The ravages of war were multiplied by smallpox, measles and other diseases from Europe. Epidemics decimated peoples who lacked all immunity. The net result was that within a century of the arrival of the first Europeans, the Indians had ceased to be a power in the entire northern spur of the Andes, running from the Pacific to the Caribbean, the area making up much of modern-day Colombia and Venezuela.

THE explorers were no less responsible than the slavers for breaking the power and destroying the culture of the Indians. Men of incredible vigor and daring, they thrust inward from all directions toward what turned out to be a vast mountain valley, green and fertile, 9,000 feet above sea level and 450 miles from the coast. One major expedition set out in 1536 from Coro, a coastal settlement east of Maracaibo. It was led by Nikolaus Federmann, an employee of the German banking house of Welser, to whom Emperor Charles V had given the right to conquer and settle Venezuela in return for a loan he and his Holy Roman Empire desperately needed. Starting from the tropical coast with 400 men, Federmann struck directly south through the mountains to the upper tributaries of the Orinoco. He then turned west and led his men through a 13,000-foot-high mountain pass. Federmann succeeded in reaching the fertile highland valley, but the whole trip had taken him too long—three years. Gonzalo Jiménez de Quesada had already arrived.

Quesada was a successful Spanish lawyer who, at the age of 35, had made the mistake of accepting an appointment as chief justice of Santa Marta on the Caribbean coast. He found Santa Marta a pesthole and resolved to lead an expedition inland. Quesada was the quintessence of the conquistador, a determined, practical man who nonetheless dreamed mad dreams even in his waking hours—restless, brave and endlessly ambitious. Laying aside his judicial robes, he led 800 men into the steaming jungle of the lower Magdalena and several hundred miles later stumbled on an Indian trail up a steep pass of the Andes. Quesada and his men pulled their supplies and each other up the cliffs with ropes and raised their surviving 59 horses in slings. Of the 800 who left Santa

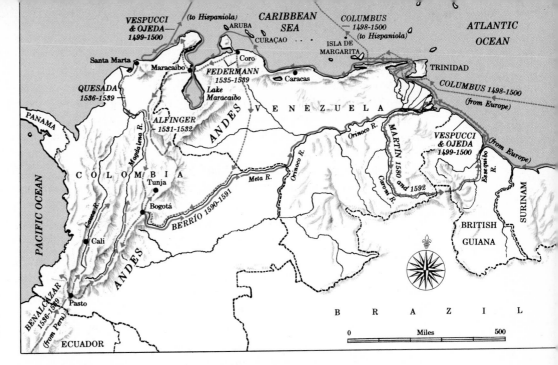

BRAVE JOURNEYS that opened up northern South America are indicated on the map at right. First to arrive was Christopher Columbus, who saw the Venezuelan coast. Amerigo Vespucci and Alonso de Ojeda, according to some accounts, sailed nearly to Colombia's present-day Santa Marta. Ambrosio Alfinger reached the Andes before he was killed by Indians. Explorations by Gonzalo Jiménez de Quesada, Nikolaus Federmann and Sebastián de Benalcázar led to the founding of Bogotá. A century after the discovery of the New World, Antonio de Berrio and Juan Martín met on the Venezuelan island of Margarita, first seen by Columbus.

Marta only 166 survived to march into the broad highland savanna where they were to build a city and name it Santa Fé de Bogotá. They found peaceful villages surrounded by the cultivated fields of the Chibcha Indians, people who mined salt deep in the mountain and whose chiefs decorated their wooden huts with gold disks and themselves with emeralds. Quesada quickly conquered the Chibchas and settled down to enjoy the spoils of victory. As before, the Indians' lives were not much valued in the face of the greed excited by their treasures.

Quesada's first visitors, six months later, were Federmann and his 160 emaciated followers. And very shortly a third group appeared from the other direction, the southwest. The leader of this expedition, Sebastián de Benalcázar, according to some chroniclers, had sailed with Columbus, helped Balboa discover the Pacific and followed Pizarro to Peru. He had also, according to some accounts, been named Governor of Quito in present-day Ecuador, but finding administration dull he had struck off north in search of El Dorado, founding Popayán and Cali before reaching the Bogotá plateau.

So many conquerors and so much wealth in gold and emeralds created a ticklish situation. Quesada, a shrewd lawyer, persuaded his visitors to leave the division of the spoils to the King, who had commissioned all three expeditions. He then went to Europe to spend some of his emeralds and have himself confirmed as Marshal of Bogotá. His appointment was slow in coming from the Spanish court, and Quesada

wandered through Europe for more than 10 years. Finally the appointment was confirmed, and he returned to Bogotá in 1550. But still his questing soul could not rest. In his old age he undertook one more search for El Dorado, whose supposed location had by then shifted toward the upper reaches of the Orinoco and the Amazon.

Had Quesada's restless energy and mad dreams achieved nothing else, he would be remembered as the figure who probably inspired one of man's great fictional creations, Cervantes' Don Quixote. But in fact he did as much as any man to explore and settle the forbidding northern tier of South America. His city, Bogotá, prospered and became the capital of a province called New Granada, with jurisdiction over the present republics of Ecuador, Colombia, Panama and Venezuela.

The Indians of the highlands did not fare quite so badly as did those of the coast. The fertile mountain valleys had relatively high concentrations of population, and those willing to work were eagerly recruited by the Spaniards as a labor force. At times the working conditions were shameful, especially where there were mines. On the great estates, too, they were victimized by cruel overseers. Large numbers of them, nevertheless, survived and were gradually incorporated into the Spanish culture, forming the basis of the modern population of both Colombia and Venezuela. The process of incorporation was facilitated by the wholesale intermarriage of Spanish men and Indian women. Not all Spaniards by any means approved of the treatment of the Indians. Bartolomé de Las Casas spent a long lifetime in many of the new lands working for them. He and others had the legal status of the Indians spelled out. The basic institution created to protect them was the encomienda. It introduced the European feudal relationship of lord and vassal. The Indians were to be brought together in villages where they would be under the authority of a Spaniard. They were not slaves but free men in the eyes of the law, entitled to certain rights in return for specified services. The Spaniard undertook to "convert, civilize and educate" them, and he guaranteed them possession of the lands owned by the village. In return, they had to work in his fields or mines.

In practice, there was nobody to see that the Spaniards carried out their part of the bargain. In spite of the protests of Las Casas and other missionaries, and in spite of the frequent renewal of the decrees and removal of legal loopholes, the Spaniards gradually established rights of ownership over the village lands and reduced the Indians to effective slavery.

IN his concern for the Indians, Las Casas encouraged the trade in Negro slaves. He may have been right in judging this a lesser evil, though he himself subsequently regretted what he had done. The Negroes stood up better to hard work in the tropics. In addition, those brought to the mainland had already been torn irreparably from their homes in Africa and shifted to the islands. But it was still an evil. A missionary who was subsequently canonized, St. Peter Claver, and others had to fight for them as Las Casas had fought for the Indians. In general, nevertheless, they were better off in Spanish colonies than in English. It was easier to win freedom, and the slave as such had legal rights.

Importation of Negroes to the mainland began early, but labor needs remained small for a century. It took that much time for reason or disillusionment to persuade the Spaniards that the best way to make a living, if not a fortune, was to settle on the land. One of the first large importers of Negro labor was the Welser bank, which had employed the explorer Federmann. The bank got a permit to import 4,000 Negroes to work on its Venezuelan grants in 1528, but this was apparently a greater number than the economy could absorb. Even in 1610, when Peter Claver reached Cartagena, the city had only 3,000 or 4,000 Negroes. Tobacco and cacao, however, were becoming important as commercial crops, and they soon created a demand for more and more field hands. The principal need for labor was along the Caribbean and Pacific coasts, where Indians were not numerous even before their decimation by disease and slave raiders. On these coasts the Negroes still retain certain of the cultural patterns, beliefs and customs of their African ancestors.

SETTLEMENT of the interior followed the traditional disposition of the Spaniards. In their homeland the Spaniards lived on high plateaus. Many of Spain's important cities lay far inland, not connected by navigable rivers to the sea. Remote places did not perturb them if these places had precious metals or cultivable land and plentiful labor.

The savanna of Bogotá fulfilled all specifications. Bogotá became the capital and a major settlement, and so it has remained, even though communications with the outside were slow and costly until the advent of the airplane. Popayán and Cali, founded by Benalcázar during the search that led him to Bogotá, similarly prospered.

Farther east, in Venezuela, settlement followed a like pattern. Valencia, founded in 1555, is 35 miles from the Caribbean coast. It had many claims to emerge as the capital and was, in fact, the temporary capital on two occasions. It is centrally located and surrounded by rich agricultural country, but its lake was bordered by disease-breeding marshes. Caracas, built 12 years later at a height of 3,000 feet in a mountain valley, soon outstripped Valencia. Most other towns were similarly sited along the line of the Andes in the north and northwest. Settlement of the lowlands was hardly worth the effort before the introduction of modern medical and agricultural techniques.

All land was vested in the Spanish Crown, and ownership was based on Crown grants. The law prescribed that land actually occupied by Indians was to remain in their possession and that they should be given more land if what they owned was inadequate for their needs. Only what was left over was available for distribution to Spaniards, and precise limits were placed on the amount any individual might own. Such was the law, but the practice was quite different. Lands were not surveyed, boundaries were vague, and the decision was often made by the interested party. The powerful and the wealthy rapidly amassed huge tracts of the best land in the vicinity of the cities, allotting small plots to their Indians on which to build huts and grow food. Political power, prestige and wealth were concentrated in the hands of the estate owner. The many who worked for him lived at a subsistence level and were completely at his mercy. It was a situation very similar to that in Spain itself and elsewhere in Europe following the breakdown of the feudal system. It was to survive almost unchanged into the 20th Century. Today it is dying out in Venezuela but continues to show remarkable vitality in Colombia.

Near the great estates the common soldiers received small farms, generally on poorer land on the mountain slopes. They married Indian women and produced the mixed strain that forms the basis of the area's current population. They were hardy and industrious people, but their opportunities were limited by the unequal distribution of the land and by the absence of outlets for their surplus labor. In the plains they became the tough *llaneros*, or cowboys, who for centuries supplied the fighting forces for revolutions and counterrevolutions.

MISSIONARIES from Spain spread out during the 16th and 17th Centuries among the Indians scattered between and beyond the settlements. Each mission post became a kind of encomienda, and the missionaries also encouraged the Indians to build villages nearby. But neither the Capuchins, working inland along the Orinoco from Cumaná, nor the Jesuits on the plains produced lasting results. The Jesuit missions were suppressed by Spain in the middle of the 18th Century. The others declined during the Wars of Independence, some Indians being absorbed by neighboring estate owners, others reverting to their traditional ways.

The European nations who cared to compete with Spain and Portugal over their South American possessions found that their best bet lay in exploring the intricate waterways of the hot and swampy Guiana area, passed over by both Spaniards and Portuguese in favor of healthier and more profitable regions. The Dutch, the English and the French had also heard rumors of a city of gold in the interior, and some dreamers hoped that the murky rivers they discovered would eventually lead them there. But most of these northern European explorers eschewed dreams of gold for the realities of commerce.

The Dutch especially were interested in any type of potential trade and ventured far inland looking for things with commercial value. A spirit of cooperation among these three nations characterized the early days of settlement and colonization; the Dutch and English together formed the first permanent settlement in the Guianas in 1616 and the French followed suit shortly thereafter. Cultivated plots sprang up along the riverbanks as far as 50 miles upstream. In both British and Dutch Guiana, tobacco, cotton, coffee and cacao were grown. The region now called Surinam had 500 plantations by 1665. By this time slaves were being imported in large numbers, and Negroes soon constituted a large segment of the population.

CONTROL of the Guiana settlements changed with the fortunes of war and shifting alliances, and 1667 found the Dutch capturing the then British possession of Surinam, which they retained in exchange for their own colony of New Netherland— later called New York. The French held onto their claim with little interference, but attempts at large-scale colonization failed, and French Guiana soon gained an infamous reputation as a disease-ridden pesthole populated largely by convicts and deportees.

In the 18th Century, circumstances forced the Guianas to bend their agricultural efforts to the production of sugar, which grew best along the coastal marshlands; this led to a gradual abandoning of the inland plantations and a concentration of the population along the coast and in the cities. However, the abolition of slavery in the 19th Century dealt a severe blow to the economy of the area, which had been heavily dependent on slave labor. The large-scale introduction of Asiatics was one of the measures taken to relieve the crisis. Other workers were brought in from a dozen other parts of the globe, with the result that Surinam and British Guiana have perhaps the most exotic mixtures of racial and ethnic strains to be found anywhere on earth.

SUPERB GOLD MASK with giant round earrings is a precious relic of the Calima Indian culture. The Calima Indians lived in the Colombian Andes centuries before the Spanish conquest.

Isolated Pockets of Primitive Life

When the Spanish and other Europeans arrived in northern South America they found Indian peoples with widely varying ways of life. Isolated by the region's rugged landscape of mountains, rivers and swamps, these native groups had developed different customs, religions and languages. Some were primitive nomads; others lived in settled communities and were excellent artisans. The conquerors imposed their languages and ways of living on the Indians. But the terrain foiled efforts at unification and even today many of the people—Indians, Negro ex-slaves and those with mixed racial backgrounds—still live in isolated and backward communities.

GREAT STONE RELICS of the Fifth Century San Agustín Indians are preserved in southern Colombia. The statues show Indian gods; the basins *(foreground)* were apparently for rituals.

FIERCE INDIAN WAR GODS dominate the ancient San Agustín relics *(opposite)*. The two figures in the taller, distinctive "double-self" statue are aspects of the same god.

INDIANS AND NEGROES, some living in a tribal state, maintain their old ways despite contact with the outside world

YOUNG BUSH NEGRO, member of a people descended from escaped slaves, stands alone in a Surinam village *(above)*. The Bush Negroes re-established African tribalism in the interior.

SEMI-WESTERNIZED TRIBESMEN who come from a Bush Negro village in Surinam *(below)* wear gaily colored garments topped off with incongruous fedora hats and carry umbrellas.

BLUE-ROBED WOMAN walks in front of a Venezuelan housing project built for Indians. Her garment, a Mother Hubbard, was brought by the Spanish, but the green pompoms are Indian.

SOMBER OYANA INDIANS, who live on the southern borders of Surinam and French Guiana, stare impassively *(opposite)* at some white visitors to their isolated jungle community.

A RURAL FARM WORKER, Miguel Zerpa, aided by his young nephew *(above)*, loads his donkey with the tops of sugar cane. The owner of the land permits local field hands such as Zerpa to use the cane tops to feed their animals. Zerpa works for several landowners south of Venezuela's Lake Maracaibo. He pays about $15 of his minimal wages each month to rent his house.

MESTIZOS of mixed white and Indian heritage perform tasks little changed in centuries

DYEING WOOL, a mestizo worker in a primitive Venezuelan blanket concern stirs an old iron kettle. The owner of the business raises her own sheep for the wool.

OPERATING THE LOOM at the blanket shop, a worker produces a finished blanket *(right).* The ancient equipment has been used for a number of generations.

STRETCHING YARN, a laborer winds strands around and around a wooden rack *(below).* This blanket concern supports two families plus several workers.

RANCH LIFE on the torrid Venezuelan plains combines rough work and extreme isolation

INDUSTRIOUS FOREMAN, Jesús Dávila of the Los Blancos ranch finishes up his accounts before dawn *(right)*. The vast Venezuelan plains lie on both sides of the Orinoco and stretch on into Colombia.

A TOUR OF THE RANCH is taken by Dávila and the ranch's absentee owner, Marcos Antonio Carpio, who has arrived for a periodic inspection. Carpio's comparatively small ranch covers 11,000 acres.

A FRIENDLY DISCUSSION between Carpio, a neighboring rancher, and Dávila is held in the welcome shade of two trees. The plains swelter in 80° to 90° heat and regularly suffer both droughts and floods.

A HEARTY DINNER prepared by the ranch's cook *(opposite, far right)* is enjoyed by Dávila and his cowboys. Ranch hands eat well, but the work is hard, the life dull, and most want to move to a city.

FLOUR SACKS sent by CARE are transformed into clothing in the tailor shop *(above)* of the Capuchin Fathers' mission school at Puerto Asís, a Colombian village near Ecuador.

MIDMORNING MEAL is served to the boys from the tailor shop *(above)*. The school, set up in 1912, has about 750 pupils from the area. About 220 of them board at the school.

GAME OF MARBLES is followed earnestly in the schoolyard *(below)*. The mission is in the plains and jungle area that contains 60 per cent of Colombia's land but 2 per cent of its people.

A JUNGLE MISSION *brings education to children in remote southern Colombia*

CONDUCTING A CLASS, Father Miguel S. Junent de Vich instructs fourth- and fifth-grade girls. The school's two priests are the only clergymen serving 18,000 people in Puerto Asís and surrounding villages. The school also has six nuns on its staff. While most of the children in the isolated region receive some education, the vast majority do not go beyond the third grade.

3

The Bloody
Road to
Independence

SPAIN'S empire in America lasted longer than
most, and its end came less from internal pressures than from events elsewhere. Most obvious of
these was Spain's decline in the 18th Century, culminating in its conquest by Napoleon in the early
19th. Even before this, however, Spain took an action that produced completely unanticipated political repercussions. In 1767 it expelled the Jesuit order
of priests from all of its territories.

To people raised in the modern United States tradition of the separation of church and state, the relationship of these two powers in Spanish America
is almost incomprehensible. The Roman Catholic
Church was in effect a Government department, and

it performed functions prescribed by the state. No
cleric could go to the New World without state au-
thorization. The king named all bishops and major
Church officials, and he paid salaries to the clergy as
to other civil servants.

In return the Church enjoyed a monopoly of religion, of social welfare and of education. The state
concerned itself with the citizen's material interests,
leaving to the Church his soul and intellect. The
strange thing is that the system worked well. Education, for example, was far more highly developed in
Spain's possessions than it was in the Thirteen Colonies before the American Revolution. The Jesuits
became the leading Church agency, particularly in

higher education. In time, however, they grew so powerful that they threatened the state's primacy. They possessed great wealth and much land; they even went so far as to challenge the accepted belief that kings ruled by divine right. Portugal expelled them in the middle of the 18th Century, and the Spaniards shortly followed suit.

The result in New Granada (the Colombia and Venezuela area), as elsewhere, was to create a vacuum in higher education. Universities and seminaries in Bogotá and other cities lost some of their best professors. In the wild scramble for replacements many professorial chairs were for the first time filled by lay teachers. These new teachers lacked the clergy's enthusiasm for scholastic philosophy. Instead, they discussed with their students the new ideas of English science, French philosophy and American political theory. It was the era of the first great modern revolution, that of the Thirteen Colonies against England, and students everywhere debated the newly formulated principles with which the North Americans prefaced their Declaration of Independence and their Constitution.

THESE principles, which were and are highly radical, thus gained currency among students and intellectuals. The masses never really accepted the new teachings, such as the right of the people to revolt against their king. The true revolutionaries, those who sought complete separation from Spain, were a mere handful of educated men. But they were resolute and closely knit, and they were able to lead the people toward freedom.

At first the revolutionaries did not challenge the authority of the Spanish Crown but only the inefficiency and oppressive policies of the colonial administration. These were issues on which it was easy to get popular backing. Because of the poverty of New Granada, as compared with other parts of Spanish America, the area had always been neglected and local administration had been poor. In both Caracas and Bogotá in the second half of the 18th Century, people had rallied to the slogan, "Long live the king, death to bad government!"

Bad governors combined with Spain's persistence in outmoded policies contributed almost as much to the explosive situation as did the new gospel of liberty. Spaniards born in America—Creoles—had increased in numbers and many enjoyed university educations, but the Crown still appointed only the Spanish-born, called *peninsulares*, to key positions. This applied to the Army, to the administration, to the law courts, to the Church and to commerce. Only four of Spanish America's 170 viceroys from Columbus' discovery to 1811 were Creoles, and only 14 of 602 captains-general.

THE rising merchant class was particularly incensed by restrictions on its opportunities to make money. The Guipúzcoa Company, a Spanish concern composed mainly of Basques, was in 1728 given exclusive rights to the Venezuelan import trade. Such monopoly of trade prompted resentment similar to that which flared into the Boston Tea Party. "The name of the King, of his ministers and of all Spaniards is heard by the leaders of this country with the greatest disgust, aversion and dislike," José de Abalos reported from Caracas in 1780. Abalos, a Spanish official, said that the people regarded the Guipúzcoa Company as "the original sin which gives rise to their wrongs."

Two Venezuelans, Francisco de Miranda and Simón Bolívar, were outstanding among the leaders of the independence movement. Miranda, often called "The Precursor" or "The Morning Star of Independence," was a brilliant, many-sided man. He excelled as linguist, student of world affairs, international intriguer and lady's man. He was an officer in the Spanish Army. He fought in the American Revolution and in the French Revolution—on the winning side in both. Catherine the Great made him an honorary colonel in the Russian Army. He knew Thomas Paine and Alexander Hamilton, Thomas Jefferson, George Washington and John Adams.

Miranda at first was motivated more by hatred of Spain than by love of freedom. He felt that the Spanish had failed to give due recognition to his military genius. But once committed to the independence movement, he would not be sidetracked. He refused a dozen opportunities to follow an honorable and lucrative career, always intent on freedom for Spanish America.

London was long his residence, his rooms the headquarters for young men from his homeland, both students and exiles. They included Bolívar and Bernardo O'Higgins, son of the Viceroy of Peru and the future liberator of Chile. With them he discussed a plan that he had prepared in 1790 for the English Government. It called for the ousting of the Spaniards from South America. Spanish rule was to be replaced by that of a hereditary monarchy, modeled on that of the Inca emperors, which would be responsible to a parliament like that of England.

Miranda's efforts were conducted against the background of Napoleon's rise to power. England's primary concern was to prevent domination of Europe by Napoleon. The British accordingly boosted Miranda's hopes while Spain was allied with Napoleon, but then abruptly cooled off when Spain showed interest in coming over to the English side. At that point Miranda moved from London to New York and there, in the winter of 1805-1806, organized an expedition of three small ships and 200 adventurers. South America groans under the Spanish tyranny, he assured his followers, and will rally to freedom's cause. But he had been 20 years in exile and had created a dream with no basis in reality. Popular support did not materialize. Spain's Army and Navy quickly routed his tiny band. Miranda was lucky to escape to Trinidad, then to England once more.

What Miranda had overlooked was that to risk revolt people need a prospect of success. Such a prospect appeared two years later, in 1808, when Napoleon invaded Spain, destroying Spain's power and prestige. Miranda's pioneer efforts then quickly bore fruit. When Napoleon sent a captain-general to govern Caracas the people rioted. Imitating the action taken by several cities in Spain, the city's leading citizens formed a junta to rule in the name of the imprisoned King Ferdinand. Bogotá and other cities followed suit.

HEAD of the Caracas junta was Simón Bolívar, the same young, rich, aristocratic plantation owner with whom Miranda had talked treason in London. The junta members all belonged to a secret society similarly headed by Bolívar. It was they who forced the decisive step from loyalty to rebellion, and in July 1811 Venezuela was proclaimed an independent republic. Miranda, who had returned some months earlier, was made head of the armed forces.

Once again Miranda was ahead of his time. Few of the people joined the junta in rejecting the King. Loyalists in Caracas included the archbishop and his big following. The cities of Coro and Maracaibo to the west were jealous of the leadership of Caracas. The plainsmen of the Orinoco proclaimed themselves staunchly for the King. Soon internal dissension grew among the revolutionaries over the form of the new constitution and the allocation of top posts. A terrible earthquake in Holy Week of 1812 proved the deathblow to the junta's plans. The enemies of the republic declared the earthquake an act of God to punish the rebels, and the frightened people believed them. When the Spaniards took the offensive, many patriot troops defected to their side. To meet the crisis, the patriot leaders gave Miranda dictatorial powers and he assumed direct command of the military campaigns. But it was too late. His officers were untrained, and the troops continued to desert. The best he could do was sign a treaty with the Spanish commander guaranteeing pardon for the rank and file, and free exit from the country for the leaders.

ALL the glory seemed to depart from the revolution in the next week. Miranda fled, taking with him the treasury. His friends later said he was going to Colombia to help the revolutionaries who reportedly were succeeding there. Bolívar and his associates, however, turned on Miranda, charging that he had sold out for the money. They captured him the night before he was to board an English ship and handed him over to the Spanish troops. It was the moment the Spaniards had been awaiting for 25 years. They shipped Miranda in chains back to Spain, and there he died in jail four years later. Bolívar left Venezuela with a passport issued by the Spanish commander. His enemies said it was the price of betraying his leader.

Whatever the rights or wrongs of these episodes, on which historians will probably never agree, Bolívar now became the soul of the independence movement. The fire he had lighted in Venezuela was spreading. In Colombia, Cartagena had raised the flag of freedom and Bogotá would soon follow. Bolívar went to Cartagena, where, in 1812, the patriots welcomed him enthusiastically and soon gave him the rank of general. He was a brilliant and ruthless commander. Marching back into Venezuela, he proclaimed a "War to the Death." Every Spaniard who failed to cooperate actively with the republic, he decreed, was to be shot on sight. One atrocity inevitably created another. Before the wars ended, the toll in lives and property was appalling.

For the moment, however, these tactics were successful and Bolívar re-entered Caracas in triumph. But it was a pyrrhic victory. A savage plainsman named Boves rode out of the interior at the head of an army of horsemen to join the Spanish troops. It was brother against brother, with no neutrals and no prisoners. Not only Bolívar and his men but the terrified people of Caracas fled and dispersed through the countryside. Bolívar escaped alone to Cartagena.

Political dissension in Colombia had by this time become universal. The Cartagena to which Bolívar returned considered Bogotá a far worse enemy than Spain, and Bolívar was employed to lead a force against the inland city. After a vicious fight Bogotá surrendered, but again Bolívar's triumph was short-lived. In Europe Napoleon had fallen and Spain was once more able to send armies out to its colonies. The divided rebels did not stand a chance against the fresh troops from Spain, and Bolívar had to save himself once more by ignominious flight, this time to Jamaica.

While in Cartagena in 1812, Bolívar had issued a manifesto that is treasured as a basic document of the independence movement. One of the causes of the fall of the Venezuelan republic, he said, was the existence of "the internal factions which in truth were the deadly poison which sent the country to its grave." In Jamaica he tried to figure out ways to heal these divisions, searching the constitutional practices of the United States, England and France for a formula that would suit the character and the

---

BOLÍVAR'S FOREIGN LEGION

Although Simón Bolívar's Wars of Independence were a stirring instance of the New World's asserting itself, his success in liberating Colombia and Venezuela owed much to the presence of troops from Europe. As was the case in the American Revolution, foreigners contributed both military know-how and world prestige to Bolívar's cause. In his army were Irishmen and Englishmen who had left home because of economic depression; German veterans of the Napoleonic Wars; Spaniards who opposed their King; and also French, Italian and Polish officers. Included were the nephews of Joseph Bonaparte, former King of Naples and Spain, and Tadeusz Kosciusko, the champion of Polish independence, as well as the son of Daniel O'Connell, "Liberator of Ireland." All told, more than 4,000 foreign soldiers joined Bolívar between 1817 and 1819.

---

level of political evolution of his countrymen. To strengthen the executive, the president would be chosen for life. Popular rights would be protected by a democratically elected lower house. The interests of Bolívar's own class would be represented by a hereditary senate. All his life he would continue to juggle constitutions, seeking a magic way to weld his fellow Creoles and the rest of the people into a coherent social unit. But most of his colleagues were selfish individualists. For them a principle was good only as long as it helped them to achieve their aims. While Bolívar was in Jamaica a sudden change occurred which illustrates both the volatility and irrationality of the people with whom he had to work. The same fierce plainsmen who had chased Bolívar from Caracas in 1814 turned on their leader Boves and on Spain. Under a new and equally illiterate leader, José Antonio Páez, they raised the flag of freedom. Their headquarters was the isolated city of Angostura (today appropriately renamed Ciudad Bolívar) on the Orinoco River. Angostura's worldwide fame rests on a formula for bitters originally concocted by a local physician, but to Venezuelans it is revered as the cradle of their independence.

Joining Páez in 1818, Bolívar re-established the republic and called a conference which named him President and Commander in Chief. His earlier defeats had enlarged his horizons, and he now saw independence for Venezuela as possible only within a broader framework of continental freedom. He naturally decided that neighboring Colombia had to be liberated first.

As Hannibal had aimed at Rome, Bolívar set his sights on Bogotá. The Andes formed a barrier more impenetrable than the Alps. Apart from a contingent of English, Irish and German volunteers who were veterans of the Napoleonic Wars, his army consisted of ragged plainsmen totally unprepared for the biting cold of the highlands. Yet the army, a force of 1,300 infantry and 800 cavalry, followed Bolívar through the wilderness of jungle and plain to the headwaters of a tributary of the Orinoco, then up a snow-covered plateau to 13,000 feet and finally down toward unsuspecting Bogotá.

The Irishman Daniel O'Leary tells in his memoirs of the feats of endurance and heroism that he witnessed. The rains were unusually heavy, he recounts, and "for seven days the troops marched up to their waists in water, camping at night where they could find higher ground not covered by the floods." This was followed by four days of struggling up steep precipices to reach the plateau late in the evening. "That was a dreadful night," he wrote, "because we could not keep a fire going. There was not a single dwelling around, and the steady drizzle, accompanied by hailstones and a constant freezing wind, extinguished the open-air fires as quickly as we got them going." Exertion in the rarefied air also took its toll. "As the troops were almost naked, and most of them . . . natives of the hot plains . . . the effect of the cold and penetrating air was fatal for many." Soldiers froze in the snow or slipped to their death in the narrow passes.

Bolívar, nevertheless, drove them on. A short man with irregular features, he had "alert and penetrating eyes." He also had a will of steel, and for him men excelled themselves. The exhausted survivors of the march flung themselves on the surprised Spaniards at Boyacá. After a sharp engagement the Spanish troops fled and Bolívar's army marched in triumph into Bogotá.

OTHER events conspired to confirm the resounding victory. More volunteers from England and elsewhere arrived to join the patriot armies. American friends were outfitting privateers to roam the Caribbean and intercept Spanish shipping. The winds of freedom were blowing in Spain itself. Liberals had revolted and urged the freeing of the colonies. Soldiers ordered to America had mutinied on the docks. Only one major Spanish army remained in the field in Venezuela, and Bolívar crushed it at Carabobo in June 1821. Except for isolated detachments of Spanish troops the entire northern segment of South America was free. A conference called the Congress of Cúcuta proclaimed the area a single state, named it Gran Colombia, and made Bolívar President and Commander in Chief.

Gran Colombia's southern frontiers remained uncertain until 1822 when José Antonio de Sucre, a brilliant general under Bolívar's command, defeated a loyalist army at Pichincha, thus freeing Ecuador from Spanish rule and adding it to the confederation. Patriot armies commanded by the Argentine General José de San Martín had simultaneously been moving north from Argentina and Chile, leaving only Peru as the last outpost of Spanish power. It took Bolívar and Sucre a further two years to complete its liberation.

AS a student in Rome, Bolívar had one day sworn on the Aventine Hill that he would "never allow my hands to be idle nor my soul to rest until I have broken the shackles which chain us to Spain." He had kept his oath. Independence was everywhere an established and irreversible fact. Unfortunately, however, there was no agreement on how to use it. Bolívar himself, although an admirer of British and U.S. democracy, had become so soured by his dealings with his fellow countrymen that he no longer believed democracy would work in South America. Analyzing the failure of the first Venezuelan republic while an exile in Jamaica in 1815, he wrote that until "our compatriots acquire the political talents and virtues which distinguish our brothers of the North, entire popular systems, far from being beneficial, will—I very much fear—come to be our ruin."

Bolívar rejected the idea of a unified Spanish South America. The area would, he believed, prove unwieldy as a single state. He equally feared the fragmentation into small units which did occur, and which in his lifetime threatened to go even further than it finally did. He could have drawn Peru and Bolivia into his Gran Colombia, but he never tried. He was satisfied that the area he ruled was adequate, and he hoped that the region from Peru to Argentina would someday coalesce into another republic.

His concrete solution for his country's political ills was a strong central government. As dissensions and divisions grew, he reacted by constantly adding to the powers of the executive. Those who favored a loose federation of cities rather than a centralized state fought back, and by 1828 most of his colleagues were in open conflict with him. At the Convention of Ocaña they refused to approve his proposed constititional changes. His reaction became a model for subsequent Latin American strongmen. He abolished the constitution and assumed dictatorial powers.

The absurdity of the situation could hardly have been greater. Those now backing the Liberator were the *godos,* the reactionary elements who had supported Spain against him to the bitter end. For them he suppressed the city councils, clamped censorship on the press, imposed a dogmatic program of studies on the schools and universities, and outlawed the Freemasons whom he had headed and who had played a decisive part in the revolt against Spain.

It was a dead end, but fortunately Bolívar had the greatness to realize it. He resigned his post in the hope that tensions would lessen. Instead, they increased. Sucre, chosen to succeed him, was assassinated almost immediately. All that Bolívar could see was mounting chaos, and he did not have the will to engage again in war between brothers. He is reported to have observed that "those who have served the revolution, have plowed the sea."

Timely warning from Manuela Sáenz, his mistress, alone saved Bolívar from the fate that had overtaken Sucre. He escaped a group of assassins by jumping from a window and hiding under a bridge. He decided to abandon the country in which "neither faith nor truth" remained. Going down the Magdalena River from Bogotá to the coast, he caught a cold that aggravated the tuberculosis he had contracted during the campaign in Ecuador. Death came in Santa Marta on December 17, 1830. He was 47.

BOLIVAR blamed "the chaos of passions," the excessive individualism inherited from Spain, for his own ruin and the death of his dreams. Actually, there were deeper, underlying realities that conspired to the same end. When the Thirteen Colonies achieved independence many of the inhabitants were trained in the operations of government and were ready to assume the responsibilities of freedom. The Creoles, always excluded from positions of power, had no such training. Further, the Thirteen Colonies had a viable, working economy and effective governmental institutions, and these continued to function

when the colonial power, Britain, was expelled. The situation was very different in South America. Gran Colombia might look very well on a map, but the territory had not even been effectively occupied. Venezuela had less than three quarters of a million people, two per square mile, and Colombia was equally empty. The social reality was a series of isolated human islands lacking common economic interests or a sense of common purpose.

THE islands themselves, such cities as Caracas, Cartagena and Bogotá, were far from a condition of internal cohesion, of self-identification as communities. Elimination of the Spanish-born ruling class, the *peninsulares,* lifted the Creoles to the top of the pile, and the mestizos found themselves in second instead of third place. But the social gap between the mestizos and the upper class did not narrow, and their living conditions improved little. Instead, the disruption of agriculture, mining and trade caused by the wars left the entire economy at a low ebb for half a century. The Creole patriots had courted the mestizos, peons and slaves during the war when soldiers were needed, but their promises were quickly forgotten after victory was achieved.

Only the slaves obtained a significant benefit. Bolívar's Congress of Cúcuta declared in 1821 that henceforth the children of slaves were free at birth. The worldwide antislavery movement was just then gaining momentum, and Latin America was swept along. The concrete change in the condition of the Negro was, nevertheless, not great. His status became the same as that of the Indian peon, tied to an employer by debt and by the lack of alternative opportunity. Social stratification continued to make it impossible for members of all these groups to climb upward by individual merit and effort. The most they could hope for was to attach themselves to some political leader and share the largess he distributed when he fought his way to power.

Man cannot live without a glimmer of hope, and for the masses in this society only two wayward rays in the intervening years have broken arbitrarily through the heavy clouds of their existence—the lottery and the coup d'état. Such social rigidity is political instability institutionalized. And it is an institution that stubbornly resists all efforts at reform.

Four members of a prominent Colombian family sit in the patio of their 35-year-old Spanish-Moorish-style mansion in Cartagena.

Persistent Signs of a Rich Spanish Heritage

Spanish influence on the lives of people in Colombia and Venezuela did not die with the end of Spanish rule. Evidence of its continuing impact is omnipresent. The old Spanish sport of bullfighting is still a national pastime in Colombia; even in the more modern Venezuela, Spanish architecture and decoration predominate in many new homes. Moreover, the old mansions and churches of the colonial period are preserved with much the same devotion that prominent Southerners in the United States show for

their antebellum homes and gardens. These outward manifestations of Old World influence have a deep-rooted significance for the region's fabric of life since they are tangible reflections of old social institutions—such as strong family ties, rule by an elite, the protection of women—that have survived into modern times. To many Colombians and Venezuelans, however, they are mere vestiges of a spirit that is disappearing as new ideals of nationalism, based on industrial progress and political liberty, take hold.

A SPACIOUS LIVING ROOM in a still-inhabited Bogotá mansion built in the 1600s epitomizes the spare elegance of Spanish décor *(above)*. Once the home of the famous Colombian poet Luís Carlos Lopez, the house is now shared by a lady named Maria Cristina Tono and her sister. The tiled floor, thick walls and shutters are features which have been employed in many modern Bogotá homes.

A GRACIOUS COURTYARD seen through wooden grillwork *(below)* is one of six in the Tono house. The house is built so that the rooms face inward on patios, a common practice of colonial architecture.

A PROTECTED BEDROOM in the Tono house is guarded with iron bars *(below)*. The purpose of the bars was twofold: to protect the ladies of the household from too-rash suitors and to ward off burglars.

A MODERN MANSION designed in the colonial style *(above)* belongs to Dr. Mauro Továr of Caracas. The archway and tiled floors are characteristic of old Spain, but the cosmopolitan nature of the decorations and the modern pieces of furniture reflect a desire of the Venezuelan upper classes to keep in touch with what is stylish in present-day Europe and the United States.

51

WATCHING THE COMPETITION, Pepe Cace-
res, Colombia's foremost bullfighter *(above, second from left),* comments on the performance of
another matador. Caceres fought the next day.

SURROUNDED BY ADMIRERS, including his
wife and infant daughter, Caceres *(below, in bed)*
tries to relax on the morning of his bullfight.
A matador since 1956, he earns $4,000 per fight.

*A BRAVE MATADOR, Pepe
Caceres is idolized in
Colombia, where bullfights
arouse a Spanish-style fervor*

READY FOR BATTLE, Caceres stands defiantly
in the ring *(above).* A few minutes later he was
gored and rushed to a hospital with a 10-inch-
deep wound. It was the 13th goring of his career.

BACK IN ACTION after two weeks in the hospital and a period of convalescence, Caceres gets
into shape by fighting a cow at a ranch *(opposite).* Cows used in training are never killed.

Freedom's Growing Pains

IN one respect at least, Simón Bolívar was right in his judgment of the compatriots he had led to freedom. They were unable or unwilling to operate a democratic system of government. As he had anticipated, they were destined to be ruled and misruled by a succession of strongmen.

In Venezuela the line of dictators has been almost unbroken, starting with Bolívar himself and passing through José Antonio Páez, José Tadeo Monagas, Juan Crisóstomo Falcón, Antonio Guzmán Blanco, Cipriano Castro and Juan Vicente Gómez. The most recent, Marcos Pérez Jiménez, was ousted only in 1958. Colombia has given more thought to appearances, especially in the 20th Century. The only open

dictator since 1903 was Gustavo Rojas Pinilla, who ruled from 1953 to 1957. But the reality has often differed little from that of Venezuela. "It is not merely a theory," as one Venezuelan historian has put it, "that there must be a sort of policeman at the top to keep everyone in order, this is the actual reality of what has happened."

One good reason why democracy failed to put down roots in 19th Century Colombia and Venezuela was that the people who could have planted and tended it had no wish to do so. The Creoles, the native-born white upper class, had won themselves a monopoly of political power by eliminating the Spanish Crown and the Spanish-born whites who had headed the colonial administration. Their individualism and aristocratic bias kept them from sharing this authority. They prevented the growth of the broad-based political organizations and labor unions with which Europe and the United States gave substance to their democratic forms. A feudal paternalism continued to characterize the Creoles' dealings with their fellow citizens.

They had used France's revolutionary concepts to justify their own rebellion against Spain, and they continued to pay lip service to these ideas. In their hearts, nevertheless, they clung to the earlier European idea of an aristocratic society in which a few are equipped and entitled to rule, while the function of the many is to obey. The basic concepts on which the United States built its system of government were equally unacceptable to the politicians of all persuasions. They did not believe that men are created equal and endowed with inalienable rights, and still less that governments derive their just powers from the consent of the governed.

IN deference to the democratic principles they proclaimed, the Creole aristocrats had to accord the people some function in the processes of government. As the aristocrats saw it, however, this function had to be clearly defined and limited. The device they hit upon was to establish a distinction between the notions of the "people" and the "nation." The distinction might best be expressed in an analogy: the "people" form the country's body but the "nation" is its soul. The people were important, of course, but it was the nation that made decisions, that expressed itself through the organs of government. It all sounded very plausible. In addition, it was most convenient for those who controlled the organs of government.

The distinction was established, with Bolívar's approval, at the constituent Congress of Cúcuta in 1821. This congress, which confirmed the union of Venezuela, Colombia and Ecuador, also wrote a Constitution that declared that sovereignty resided in this mystical thing called the nation. The people, on the other hand, were not to "exercise any other attribute of sovereignty than that of taking part in primary elections." Two other provisions further circumscribed the people's exercise of sovereignty.

Provincial assemblies, not the people directly, were to elect the president and vice president. The people were to elect Congress, but only those among them who owned property could vote.

Bolívar's plan for a single nation of Gran Colombia never really got off the drawing board. A separatist party led by José Antonio Páez formed in Venezuela almost at once, and soon Colombia was also split, one faction favoring Bolívar, another backing the local patriot, Francisco de Paula Santander. But the question of what class should exercise power was never at issue. The Creoles fought among themselves simply to determine which of them should occupy the top place.

When Gran Colombia broke up into separate republics, both of the new states of Colombia and Venezuela wrote themselves new Constitutions. But these documents and the many rewritings that followed throughout the century remained faithful to the spirit of the Constitution of Cúcuta in limiting the role of the people in political life. Practice went even further. Whether the franchise was narrower or broader, according to the whim of the drafter, all that the voters were allowed to do was to rubber-stamp the decisions of their betters. Only 319 votes were cast in a Presidential election in Venezuela in 1847, while 239,708 electors exercised the franchise 25 years later. But in both cases the result was the same. The 1847 election gave the Presidency to the man already agreed upon by the party leaders and approved by Congress. The election 25 years later, in 1872, converted a dictator into a "constitutional" President, giving him all but 17 of the votes cast.

THE 20th Century has seen a progressive extension of the franchise. All Venezuelans over 18 and all Colombians over 21 now have the right to vote. Their ability to influence the political process nevertheless remains limited, particularly in Colombia. In both countries lists of candidates are drawn up by the self-perpetuating party leaderships. The voter therefore never has a chance to vote for a man not thoroughly acceptable to the party. The concern of the individual deputy, therefore, is not to please his constituents but to satisfy the party bosses who decide whether to include him on the list. The deputy need not, and often does not, live in his constituency. The voter's own choice is further restricted by the traditional nature of his party allegiance. His grandparents or great-grandparents were either Conservatives or Liberals because the upper-class family to which they were tied by social and economic bonds had made the choice for them. Only since World War II have Venezuelans begun to break away from these commitments. Colombians still feel bound by them.

The reasons that impelled the members of the upper class, in the second quarter of the 19th Century, to split into Conservatives and Liberals were often arbitrary, although the issues themselves were real enough. The Conservatives supported a strong centralized state, they were churchgoers, and they sought to maintain the Roman Catholic Church in the privileged position it had enjoyed in colonial times. The Liberals were states' righters, seeking a loose form of federal association and a weak central government. While not formally rejecting Roman Catholicism, they were often Freemasons and seldom if ever went to church. And they advocated measures to limit the Church's power. They wanted in particular to substitute a state monopoly of education for that previously enjoyed by the Church.

The first of these issues to be debated was that of centralism versus federalism. As early as the Constitution of Cúcuta in 1821, sides were being taken. Most Venezuelans objected to the idea of being ruled by Bogotá, and they wanted Gran Colombia itself to have a federal form of government. At Cúcuta, Bolívar's influence enabled him to win support for a centralist state. Only seven years later, however, the federalists had grown so strong that they rejected his request to the Convention of Ocaña to strengthen the central Government further. The result was the collapse of Gran Colombia.

THE FERMENT FROM FREEMASONRY

Freemasonry, a movement that played a major part in the Colombian-Venezuelan fight for independence, has its origins in medieval England. Originally the term signified associations of itinerant craftsmen who worked in stone. They met to discuss business and the news of the day. By the 17th Century permanent lodges had been set up in Scotland and England, secret rituals had been adopted, and aristocrats were joining. In the 1700s lodges were built all over Europe, Asia, America and the West Indies, and men from all walks of life were meeting to profess belief in God and adherence to liberty, equality and progress. Such talk naturally led at times to revolutionary ferment. In 1796 several Spanish Freemasons undertook an unsuccessful revolution in Venezuela. By the early 1800s lodges had been formed on Venezuelan soil. And, as had been the case in France and America, when revolution finally came, many leading figures were Freemasons.

All vital factors at this time seemed to favor regional autonomy. The new nations that resulted from the dissolution of Gran Colombia consisted of widely separated cities, each with a history of self-reliance and of resistance to the claims of Bogotá and Caracas to rule them. They did not depend on the two capital cities for their trade, and communications remained slow and difficult. Nevertheless, the end result in both countries was a highly centralized system. Colombia abandoned even the forms of federalism in the Constitution of 1886. Venezuela retains the appearance of having autonomous states, but in practice it is equally centralistic.

This does not mean that the Conservatives imposed their will in either country. Instead, the solution was a pragmatic one, and both parties had a hand in finding it. As Bolívar had believed and argued, the divisive forces were so strong that federalism would have led to fragmentation. However, each time that this threatened, a dictator arose and broke the centrifugal forces. Whether he was a Conservative or a Liberal, the logic of his position forced him to set up a strong executive in the capital. If he happened to be a Liberal, he continued to insist that he was strengthening the federal system. But the politicians knew that this was only a game. One political leader, Antonio Leocadio Guzmán, admitted as much, telling the Venezuelan Congress with disarming frankness in 1867 that his friends and he had used the slogan of federation simply to gain power. "For if our opponents, gentlemen, had said *Federation,* we should have said *Centralism.*"

The issue of centralism versus federalism was thus solved as the 19th Century progressed, with centralism the victor. The place of the Church in society proved harder to establish. The revolutionary leaders Miranda and Bolívar, and many of their associates, were advocates of religious toleration. However, the Venezuelan Constitution of 1811 retained Roman Catholicism as the sole state religion, and Bolívar later sought the support of the Church when he needed allies to build a strong central government and to advance a program of social reconstruction.

THE Catholic Church accordingly emerged after independence with some of the privileges, though not all, that it had enjoyed under Spanish rule. It had control of education at all levels. It operated orphanages, hospitals and other charitable institutions. It controlled the cemeteries. It made and executed marriage laws. It ran its own courts for the clergy. It retained the wealth it had accumulated, and it continued to benefit from special taxes.

The difference in attitude toward the Church on the part of the two parties was one of degree rather than of principle. They realized that political evolution called for a narrowing of the Church's sphere of activity and a corresponding extension of the powers of the state. But both parties wanted to retain the Church as an institution and both also wanted to have a close association between the Church and the state. They had looked to the United States and French Constitutions for inspiration in drafting and remodeling their basic laws, yet they could not bring themselves to imitate these countries in proclaiming a complete separation of church and state. The Conservatives believed that they could keep the Church as a junior but friendly partner. The Liberals thought it necessary to reduce it to the status of a servant.

An early conflict with the Church arose over the appointment of bishops. The Spanish Crown had always enjoyed the privilege of naming bishops in its American colonies. The new republics insisted that this privilege had passed to them with the other rights of sovereignty. The Pope was under pressure from Spain, which long continued to claim authority over what it called its rebellious colonies. In addition, the Pope wanted to end a privilege that had been conferred on the king of Spain by his predecessors. Neither side would yield, and for a considerable time few bishops were named to vacant dioceses. Finally, however, both Colombia and Venezuela reached a compromise that still continues in

force. The Pope appoints a bishop only after he has reached an agreement on the candidate with the Government of the country involved.

When Gran Colombia broke up, the Venezuelan leader was José Antonio Páez, the same illiterate plainsman who in 1818 had welcomed Bolívar at Angostura and started him on the road to final success against Spain (see Chapter 3). In the interval he had been teaching himself to read and write. He had also begun to learn the statecraft that enabled him to control the destiny of his country for 33 years, from 1830 to 1863.

Páez illustrates the artificiality of the labels in Venezuelan politics. He is called a Conservative because the group he built up around him developed into the country's Conservative Party—and because the opposition called itself Liberal. His Constitution of 1830 claimed to be federalist but was in fact centralist. And he took a strong stand against the Catholic Church. He abolished its independent tax revenues, substituting state salaries that left the clergy directly dependent on the Government, like other civil servants.

DURING most of the Páez era the dictator governed from the side lines. He was, in fact, so powerful that he was able to let the Liberal Party, which had been formed to oppose him, assume the reins of Government, while he himself continued to set the lines of Government policy. Venezuelan historian Guillermo Morón explains why this was possible. "There did not in fact exist two opposed political ideologies," he writes, "and the parties were power-seeking groups."

One of the men who became President with the approval of Páez did, however, decide that he could become the real ruler of the country. He was José Tadeo Monagas, and he and his brother actually succeeded in driving Páez into exile. Yet even from far-off New York the old dictator continued to be influential. When Monagas amended the Constitution to provide for his own re-election, a new revolution broke out and Páez returned and resumed active control.

By this time, however, Venezuela was full of private armies, and the Administration had been thoroughly undermined. Even Páez was no longer able to dominate the warring factions, and he surrendered control to one of the contenders, Juan Falcón, and went once more into exile. He left behind him a bloody civil conflict—called the Federalist War—political anarchy, national confusion and administrative chaos, and so it continued almost without interruption until a new strongman emerged. He was Antonio Guzmán Blanco, and he entered Caracas at the head of a victorious army in April 1870 to inaugurate 18 years of peace and prosperity.

Guzmán Blanco called himself a Liberal, but his philosophy was one of enlightened conservatism. A civilizer as well as an autocrat, he improved agriculture, built roads and railways, and constructed an aqueduct to carry water to Caracas.

As Grand Master of the Freemasons of Venezuela, Guzmán Blanco undertook to complete the downgrading of the Catholic Church begun by Páez, being convinced that it was necessary to secularize the country in order to modernize it. He established civil marriage, confirmed the freedom of religion and invited Protestant missionaries into Venezuela. He transferred the control of education from the Church to the state, making primary education both free and compulsory. He built many schools, primary, secondary and technical, although not enough to make the compulsory attendance clause written into the law more than a gesture. He exiled the Archbishop of Caracas for refusing to honor him in religious services, promulgated a law that forbade leaving property to the Church by will, cut payments to the clergy and even threatened to set up a national church. In the end he broke the Church's spirit and lowered its status in the eyes of the Venezuelan public.

IF the Guzmán Blanco era marks the fall of one power group, the Church, it also marks the rise of another, the Army, which would dominate Venezuelan political life for nearly a century. Armies had been important in Venezuela long before Guzmán Blanco's time, but these had been armies in which officers and men were often civilian amateurs rather than career soldiers. A more or less self-appointed general would assemble a force and, when he had achieved his objective, share the spoils of victory with his followers and allow them to go home. If his soldiers felt they had not got as much as they deserved, they were soon ready to sell their swords to another plotter, hoping to do better next time.

By the time Guzmán Blanco had come to power, however, the art of war was beginning to feel the impact of the technological revolution. Imported European equipment, especially artillery, was becoming too complex to be handled by amateurs. It was also becoming prohibitively expensive for a local leader to raise his own force. The rifle, bayonet and machete had ceased to be enough. In the future some support from the regular armed forces would be required in order to launch a rebellion.

THE political leaders were not long in coming to realize the new importance of the military. In fact, it was the generals who brought an end to the era of Guzmán Blanco in 1892 and put General Joaquín Crespo in power for six years. Some years later, Juan Vicente Gómez, dictator from 1908 to 1935, was the man who fully recognized the new role of the Army. Rather than try to fight it, he devoted his efforts to keeping it faithful to him. He put his kinsmen and henchmen into high posts to such an extent that they continued to dominate Army policy long after his death. He imposed rigorous discipline, compensating for it with high pay and special social and legal privileges for officers.

The net effect of these various developments was that Venezuela reached the end of the 19th Century without having come perceptibly closer to the high-sounding political objectives for which the Wars of Independence had been fought. The upper class retained its monopoly of political and economic initiative while making very poor use of its power. It is true that the Catholic Church's former anomalous position as a state within the state had been corrected. But instead, a new, more self-seeking and less beneficial force, the Army, was starting to dominate public life. A long road still lay ahead before Venezuela could be called a modern democracy.

Colombia during the 19th Century was concerned with much the same issues as was Venezuela and found similar solutions. The first major conflict arose over the claims of the Church to function autonomously. Liberal President José Ignacio de Márquez approached the problem very astutely by fomenting a division among the Church leaders themselves. On the ground that certain mission properties owned by religious orders were not being used for the educational and religious purposes for which they were intended, he transferred them to the parish clergy. One of the offended priests led a rebellion in 1839 which precipitated general disorder throughout the country. Márquez was, however, supported by the Archbishop of Bogotá, as well as by two outstanding generals, Pedro Herrán and Tomás Cipriano de Mosquera, both future Presidents. He succeeded in crushing the revolt and establishing the principle that the state could dispose of Church property.

DURING the following 10 years Colombia experienced the conservative and clerical reaction that was occurring in many parts of Latin America. A law of 1842 readmitted the Jesuits. The Constitution of 1843 proclaimed that the state had the duty to protect the Catholic faith. But a change of government brought a swing of the pendulum. The Constitution of 1853 proclaimed freedom of religious worship and placed Catholicism on a level with other faiths. When the Holy See in Rome protested, the Colombian Congress went even further. It declared complete separation of Church and state and then proceeded to interpret the phrase as meaning complete control of the Church by the state. In addition to once more expelling the Jesuits and abolishing a number of legal privileges hitherto enjoyed by the clergy, this regime closed many convents, monasteries and other religious houses. The seminary as a separate institution was abolished, seminarians being incorporated into the national college, where the state would maintain control over their education.

Colombian politics were so dominated by the issues of clericalism and anticlericalism that the urgent needs of the country were ignored. The politicians hardly noticed what they were doing when, in the late 1840s, they passed a bill, advocated by Colombia's merchants and landowners, that lowered tariffs on imports. British goods flooded the market, Colombian craftsmen, such as spinners and weavers, were almost ruined, and wages for labor plummeted.

Despite these economic hardships, the politicians continued to concentrate on Church matters—and

shortly managed to provoke a civil war. The revolt broke out over the Constitution of 1853, which was severely anticlerical. As before, the pendulum soon swung the other way, and in 1857 a pro-Church faction gained power and wrote a new Constitution. This document also produced unrest and upheaval since, in addition to restoring some of the Church's privileges, it sharply curtailed the power of the central Government, giving the states all powers not specifically reserved for the "confederate" power in Bogotá. This was an invitation for local strongmen to rise and seize power, and rise they did. Former President Tomás Cipriano de Mosquera, now Governor of the state of Cauca, announced in 1860 that his state was assuming full sovereign powers. Others soon followed suit and the civil war started all over again. Mosquera occupied Bogotá in 1861 and two years later he promulgated yet another Constitution. In addition to strengthening the central Government, this document confirmed a series of anti-Church measures that Mosquera had already taken by decree. The Jesuits, readmitted by the previous regime, were re-expelled and their property confiscated. All monasteries were closed and no clergyman was permitted to perform his priestly functions without permission of the civil authorities.

LIKE its predecessors, the Constitution of 1863 reflected not a national consensus but the partisanship of the victors. It could be assumed that its provocation would shortly induce a counterprovocation. That this did not happen is due primarily to the good sense and tenacity of a politician and journalist named Rafael Núñez.

Núñez had started in politics as a "socialist Radical," that is to say, a member of the extreme anticlerical faction of the Liberal Party. He became an independent, then a moderate Liberal, and finally a Right-Wing Liberal. Right-Wing Liberals in Colombia were and are something like Southern Democrats in the United States: they would feel more at home in the other party but traditional commitment keeps them where they are. As a Right-Wing Liberal, Núñez won the support of the Conservatives, as well as that of elements in his own party, and he was elected President of Colombia in 1880. Here he quickly showed his statesmanship, writing and speaking on the virtues of national unity. He urged a continued coalition of Conservatives and Right-Wing Liberals and called for religious toleration. Núñez's masterwork was the Constitution of 1886. It has been criticized as leaning far more toward Conservative than toward Liberal positions, but it was the first real attempt to find common ground, and it was so successful that later Liberal and Conservative governments continued to live with it. It was frequently amended, but its provisions formed the basic law of Colombia until 1936.

ITS great achievement was to find a solution for the Church-state problem that had kept Colombia in turmoil for 30 years. The solution was a series of elaborate compromises. The Constitution recognized the Catholic Church as the national religion and "an essential element of the social order," but not as an established church. All cults "not contrary to Christian morals or law" were authorized, and no one was to be molested because of his beliefs. The state undertook to protect the Catholic Church and to enforce respect for it and its ministers. The Church was given wide authority over education, even in state schools, including a censorship of all school texts having to do with morals and ethics. In the more remote parts of the country, the "mission territories," education was placed under its exclusive control. It did not get back its seized properties, but the state undertook to make payments in perpetuity as compensation. In addition, the Church was again authorized to receive and hold property, and property put to certain uses was to be tax exempt.

The Núñez Constitution was not only strongly centralist but also weighted to favor the president. Though it divides the public power into legislative, executive and judicial branches, it vests the executive with so much discretionary authority that the other branches are much less important than they are in the United States. This can be criticized as undemocratic. But it can also be interpreted as a concession to the authoritarian tradition of the country's rulers. The ability of the president to function as a sort of dictator *within* the constitutional system has undoubtedly helped Colombia avoid open dictatorships since the time of Núñez. Every President since that era, with the sole exception of Rojas Pinilla during the

1950s, has come to power by way of the ballot box.

Núñez also deserves credit for the fact that the Army in Colombia has played a much smaller role in politics than has the Army in neighboring Venezuela. Except for a few years at the turn of the century, the country was peaceful during the late 19th Century and the early 20th, the period during which the national Army was institutionalized. It was, in consequence, relatively free from the temptation to take sides in political quarrels, so that a tradition grew strong among the officers that the Army was above and outside politics. There has been only one major break in this tradition. In 1953 the Army installed Rojas Pinilla as dictator at a moment when irresponsible politics threatened civil chaos, and it ousted him four years later when the cure had proved worse than the disease.

The experience of four years of rule by an Army-backed dictator had its good side. The ineptitude of the Army representatives as administrators and the degeneration of the regime into tyranny caused wide disillusionment. The resistance of public opinion undoubtedly played a part in persuading the Army not to repeat the process 10 years later when new political confusion presented a similar temptation.

TO describe the Army in Colombia as normally above and outside politics is not to say that it is responsible to the president and responsive to his wishes in the same way as his civil servants. By a series of unwritten conventions it performs certain functions and enjoys certain privileges. After long study of the role of the Army in Latin American politics, Professor Edwin Lieuwen has concluded that in Colombia, "where institutional military matters are concerned the civilian authorities have no control." A sort of gentleman's agreement exists, he says. If the Government allows the armed forces to function unmolested and look after their own affairs, it need have no fear that they will seize control.

The Army exacts a heavy price for staying on its own side of the fence. A quarter of Colombia's total expenditure went to the Army and national police in the 1963-1964 budget. Nor is the situation likely to improve until the country develops a broad-based democracy in which government expresses the views and reflects the interests of all citizens.

A FISHING VILLAGE, La Boquilla rests on the water's edge along the Colombian coast *(above)*. In addition to fishing, the people live by selling sand they dig from the beaches. In this languid region hogs roam freely and the pace of life is slow.

A BUSY TOWN gets a traffic jam as a truck and a bus block a steep street in Arauca, Colombia, a trading center for a rich agricultural region. Most Colombians and Venezuelans live in such mountainous country, and the population is growing rapidly.

Three citizens of San Agustín, a village in the Colombian Andes, escape the afternoon sun beneath the eaves of old adobe houses.

Small-town Life: Midway on the Social Scale

Millions of Colombians and Venezuelans know neither the wealth and power of the traditional ruling classes nor the isolation of the peasants who live in the countryside. This middle group—for the most part still too impoverished and uneducated to be considered a middle class in the North American sense—is found in the region's many towns and villages and in the barrios, the self-sufficient local quarters of larger cities. Some, unable to find jobs, live at a bare subsistence level in noisome slums. But many think of themselves as on the way up, potential members of their country's new democratic society.

SMALLER COMMUNITIES support an active life despite their often languid appearance

A PLEASANT SHADED PLAZA offers residents of Popayán, an old town in the southern Colombian Andes, a place to rest on a hot afternoon. Long isolated, Popayán now lures many tourists.

A NEWSPAPER STAND draws a group of customers in the Venezuelan town of Naiguata *(opposite)*, a small resort on the Caribbean. On the hill above the stand is a modest residential area.

AN AIRY POOL HALL attracts young men during the siesta hour in San Agustín *(below)*, a town in the Andes. Relics of one of Colombia's ancient Indian civilizations were found nearby.

THE SUNDAY MARKET brings peasants, many of whom have donned jackets for the occasion, to the small town of Arauca in western Colombia's Cauca River valley. Arauca is a busy trading center since it is in the heart of the coffee-growing region.

65

A CHEERFUL FAMILY crowds into its small home in the Barrio Aranjuez outside Manizales. The barrio was constructed largely with funds provided by the Alliance for Progress.

A LOCAL BUS used by some of the barrio children to get to school makes its way *(right)* past the barrio's cement-block houses. The schools accommodate only a third of the children.

66

AN OUTDOOR SINK behind her house is used by a local beauty, Marta Quintero, 19-year-old runner-up in a Queen of the Barrio contest. She helps care for nine brothers and sisters.

A CORNER STOREKEEPER in the Barrio Aranjuez makes a sale *(below)*. The barrio, while far from elegant, represents a start at helping Colombia's thousands who are ill-housed.

Colombian workmen tend a coffee-toasting machine at Chinchina, a center of Colombia's large coffee industry. Six million bags are exported

annually, accounting for 70 per cent of Colombia's total exports.

5

Wealth from Coffee and Oil

ALEXANDER VON HUMBOLDT, the German naturalist, found the people as odd as their habitat when he explored the interior of Venezuela and Colombia in the early 19th Century. He was particularly scornful of Venezuela's *mantuanos*, or mantle bearers. The aristocrats were so known because archaic laws gave them the exclusive right to wear mantles and capes, silk, lace and pearls. These aristocrats, Humboldt observed, would rather lose than share their privileges. "They would prefer foreign domination to an authority exercised by inferior castes; they abhor any political constitution founded on equal rights."

The *mantuanos* had a monopoly not only of fine clothing but also of education, membership in the clergy and advancement in the Army. They proudly called themselves *blancos* (whites) and boasted of a purity of blood which not many possessed. The primary intention of the leaders of the wars of independence was to transfer power within the "white" aristocracy from those born in Spain, the *peninsulares*, to those born in the colonies, the *criollos*, or

Creoles. The lower classes found little to choose between these two sets of masters. When friction between the two groups of aristocrats began to increase at the end of the 18th Century, the lower classes understandably sought to turn the conflict to their own advantage. A free zambo (mixed Indian-Negro) led a revolt in 1795 "to inplant the law of the French," that is to say, to free the slaves and end white supremacy. But it was the *llaneros*, the mestizos of the plains of western Venezuela and eastern Colombia, who created the biggest challenge.

Humboldt, who happened to visit the plains at just the right time of year, wrote admiringly of "the sea of grass." The growing season is short, however, for the dry-season sun quickly burns the vegetation and cracks the parched earth. When the rains return, vast stretches of the plains become a shallow ocean, which then dries out to mud and malaria before the grasses sprout once more.

ONLY men of steel and muscle survived in this inhospitable land, and their temperament was as volatile as their environment. In the words of Venezuelan novelist Rómulo Gallegos, the plainsman was "indomitable and long-suffering, indolent and tireless; impulsive and wary in combat, undisciplined and loyal with his superior . . . gay and melancholy on all occasions, a realist and a weaver of fantasies, humble afoot and proud on horseback."

It was easy to arouse their animosity against the wealthy Creoles, and that was how the *llanero* leader José Tomás Boves got their support for the 1814 campaign which drove Simón Bolívar in ignominious flight from Caracas (Chapter 3). In order to win them over to the patriot side, the later *llanero* leader José Antonio Páez, who supported Bolívar, and Bolívar himself, had to promise them social and economic reform, a promise extended to all the lower-class elements, including Negroes. Specifically, veterans of the patriot armies were assured that the lands confiscated from royalist supporters would be turned over to them.

The lower classes, however, lacked the leadership and cohesion to compel fulfillment of these promises. Just as soon as the Creoles were sure of victory over Spain, they forgot the reforms they had undertaken to effect. Bolívar himself in his last years helped to confirm Colombia's wealthy Creole class in its entrenched position by throwing his weight behind the most reactionary groups. A similar process occurred in Venezuela where the Constitution of 1830 was written by a coalition of merchants and big landowners. Predictably, it voided the earlier promises of social reform and land distribution.

In Venezuela, veterans holding war-bonus certificates payable in abandoned lands found themselves stuck in administrative quagmires. Many were forced to sell their claims for practically nothing to Creole speculators who thus reconsolidated the large holdings of the *peninsulares* they had earlier vowed to break up. Laws providing for rapid foreclosures for debt further concentrated land in the hands of the few. Other laws giving the vote only to landowners completed the process, excluding the poor from having any voice in politics.

The 19th Century, accordingly, saw a strengthening of the hacienda, or big estate, as the basic socioeconomic unit of Colombia and Venezuela. The owners of these vast expanses of land, enjoying the free labor of their serfs, were absolute masters of the countryside and also exercised great power in the towns, where they spent most of their time. The farm workers were allotted small plots which enabled them to maintain themselves and their families. Their work for their masters provided a surplus which fed the towns and paid for imports.

THIS agricultural society had an extremely high level of internal stability. Nevertheless, just as the earlier Indian society had been disrupted by the shock of the Spanish invasion, so the hacienda society came under attack from outside in the second half of the 19th Century. The invasion this time was not by armed force, but by bankers and salesmen from the countries of Western Europe and North America in search of markets for their rapidly expanding industries. Opportunities for mercantile activity in Colombia and Venezuela were limited since the rural masses remained almost entirely outside the money economy. But the people in the cities welcomed the foreign manufactured goods which were less expensive than the pots and pans, the shoes and clothing produced by their own artisans. The wealthy began to import home furnishings, musical instruments and carriages. The public in the cities and towns began to demand transport, communications, street lighting, piped water and other facilities which more advanced countries had established as essential to civilized living.

The immediate result of this expanded demand for imports was a scramble for ways to pay for them. The industrial countries sought principally the metals and other raw materials required to feed their factories. But they also needed agricultural products to feed their workers. Since Colombia and Venezuela were not then able to offer industrial raw materials, other than small quantities of gold and silver, they embarked on the expansion of crops for export, especially cacao and coffee.

CLIMATE, terrain and soil characteristics combine to make coffee an ideal crop for both of these countries. Coffee trees, originally native to the highlands of Ethiopia, grow well and yield beans of high quality in the volcanic soil on the slopes of mountains between 2,000 and 6,000 feet above sea level. And because coffee is a tree crop and the earth beneath the trees need not be plowed, it is ideally suited for growing on mountain slopes, which quickly erode when planted with annual crops.

In both Colombia and Venezuela in the late 19th Century, the main concentrations of population were precisely in the areas best suited for taking advantage of this new source of income. Having explored the entire region for gold, the Spaniards had established their great estates where the Indians were most numerous. They had done so not only because they needed a labor force but also because the Indians had settled in the places with the most suitable soil and climate for living, the valleys at the middle levels of the Andes. The flat bottom lands in these valleys were staked out by the Spaniards for themselves; the mestizos were spread around them on the fringes of the mountains. It was this sloping land that turned out to be just right for coffee. Once the export trade had begun in 1835, the cultivation of coffee expanded rapidly. The peasant families were big and the younger sons established their own farms by planting trees higher and higher up the slopes. The process was halted only by the frost line, the limit for the survival of the coffee tree.

In Colombia, in particular, the coffee industry went on growing until it dominated the economy.

The effect of the expansion was to incorporate the economies of Colombia and Venezuela more fully than before into those of the Western world. Previously, rural communities had depended almost entirely on their own resources. Now the peasants produced a crop for sale and used what money they received to buy food and clothing. It was a period of national expansion. Roads, railroads and harbors were built. to encourage trade. The middlemen in the cities prospered. Between 1850 and 1880, Bogotá doubled its population from 30,000 to 60,000. By 1900 the figure had passed 100,000, and the city had "many fine hygienic new houses" and a tramway.

Some of the consequences were less favorable. The upper classes organized the coffee trade within the traditional social framework. In Venezuela, much of the coffee was grown on big estates, the principal compensation to the workers consisting of a piece of land on which to grow food and build a shack. In Colombia, the peasants as a rule grew the beans on their own account, but the big men handled the final processing, controlled market and export, and determined the price paid to the small producer. In both countries, therefore, the mass of the people continued to receive barely enough to live at a primitive level.

MEANWHILE, the upper classes themselves had their problems. The aristocrats, it turned out, were not really very good businessmen. They were crippled by the attitudes and ambitions they had inherited from Spain. Contrasting the society created by the English in the Thirteen Colonies with that created by the Spaniards, the Spanish writer Salvador de Madariaga has said that the Spaniard's ambition was to be a prince, the Englishman's to be a capitalist. The Spaniard's urge was upward, the Englishman's forward. The full impact of this difference in attitude revealed itself in the late 19th Century. While the United States shot ahead, countries like Colombia and Venezuela began to sink under the weight of the monuments raised by princelings in their own honor.

Part of the trouble stemmed from the fact that the governments and business communities of both Colombia and Venezuela were content to play the part assigned their nations by the economists of the

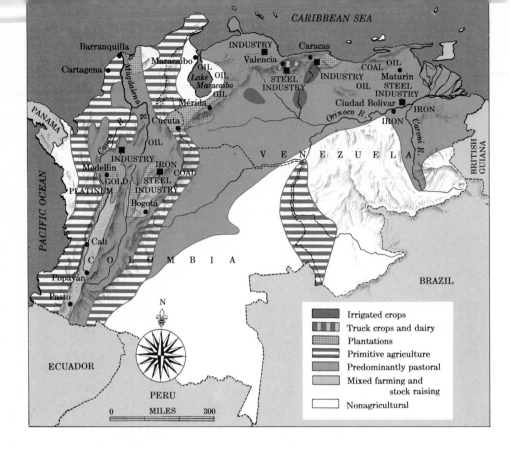

CARIBBEAN SEA

Barranquilla
Cartagena
Maracaibo
OIL
Lake
Maracaibo
OIL
OIL
Mérida
INDUSTRY
Valencia
Caracas
STEEL
INDUSTRY
INDUSTRY
COAL
OIL
Maturín
OIL STEEL
INDUSTRY
Ciudad Bolívar
IRON
IRON
Cúcuta
OIL
INDUSTRY
IRON
COAL
STEEL
INDUSTRY
Medellín
GOLD
PLATINUM
Bogotá
Cali
Popayán
Pasto

PACIFIC OCEAN
PANAMA

V E N E Z U E L A
Orinoco R.
Caroní R.
BRITISH GUIANA

C O L O M B I A

BRAZIL

N

ECUADOR

PERU

0   MILES   300

Irrigated crops
Truck crops and dairy
Plantations
Primitive agriculture
Predominantly pastoral
Mixed farming and
  stock raising
Nonagricultural

ECONOMIC ACTIVITIES are severely limited by geography in Colombia and Venezuela, as shown on the map at left. Vast sections of mountains, jungles and plains in the two countries are unsuited to any sort of agriculture. However, parts of the plains are ideal for cattle. In Colombia, coffee, the principal crop and leading export, is grown in the mild climate of the Andean slopes in the west and central part of the country. Most of Venezuela's oil—the basis of its economy—comes from Lake Maracaibo, while other important sources are found in eastern Venezuela.

time. They were satisfied to produce food and raw materials for the industrial nations and to import manufactured goods. Since labor was free on the vast estates, the owners felt no need to modernize their agricultural techniques; the unpaid workers utterly lacked purchasing power and therefore did not constitute a mass market which might have encouraged the development of local industries.

Thus the profits made by the hacienda owners and the city middlemen which should have gone into capital formation were dissipated in various forms of conspicuous consumption—in parks, squares and monuments, and in the big houses which the wealthy filled with imported furnishings.

To maintain this way of life, the ruling classes bought abroad more than they could pay for, gradually undermining the national credit. Foreign commercial interests advanced money to meet urgent obligations, but on progressively more onerous terms. Things reached such a desperate point in Venezuela that the Government had to pledge a large part of its ordinary revenues simply to meet interest payments.

To add to their problems, Colombia and Venezuela began to experience the effects of an economic "law" later formulated by the Argentine economist Raúl Prebisch. Manufactured goods exported by industrial powers tend to hold their prices even in a recession, while the prices of agricultural exports are highly sensitive to world market conditions. The demand of Colombians and Venezuelans for imported manufactures, and the cost of these goods, grew steadily from year to year, but the income from coffee and other export crops fluctuated wildly. Two years of low coffee prices in the late 1890s brought on a crisis in Venezuela's balance of payments which had immediate repercussions. Venezuela's national revenue, which totaled more than $9.5 million in 1896-1897, fell to $6.5 million the next year, recovered to $7.5 million the following year and plummeted to $5.3 million a year later. The national debt was then nearly $36.6 million, and foreign creditors were pressing for payment. Soon some of them went even further.

This was the era when big business dominated the foreign policy of the major powers, collecting commercial debts under the protection of naval guns, and Venezuela was the victim of a more than usually outrageous intervention. Lacking funds to meet its obligations, the Venezuelan Government in 1902 suspended payment of the foreign debt. Foreseeing that something like this was going to happen, U.S. President Theodore Roosevelt had made a speech some months earlier in which he gave a rather odd

72

interpretation to the Monroe Doctrine: "We do not guarantee any state against punishment if it misconducts itself. . . ." This was taken to mean, naturally enough, that the U.S. would not object if Venezuela's creditors tried to collect by force. Germany and Britain moved fastest. A joint naval force appeared off the Venezuelan coast and captured the Venezuelan Navy—"four little boats smelling of rust, bananas, stew and *mestizo* sweat."

The British followed this by bombarding some coastal forts and, adding insult to injury, by kidnaping 20 pedigreed fighting cocks during a foray ashore. Venezuelan President Cipriano Castro, whose initial reaction had been to jail all the British and German nationals he could find, now pleaded that some sort of arbitration be arranged. Britain and Germany were cool to this proposal at first but eventually agreed to submit the problem to the Hague Court of Permanent Arbitration. By this time the claims had swollen to many times their original size, and although the arbitrators scaled them down, they found in general for the claimants, inflicting a harsh blow on Venezuela's pride and treasury alike.

At about the same time, Colombia was experiencing an even more severe humiliation—the loss of Panama, its northernmost province. United States naval strategists had decided to complete the canal across the isthmus which had been started by a French company. Unable to reach a satisfactory agreement with Colombia's leaders, they promoted the secession of Panama, and Colombia lacked the power to do more than protest.

INTERNALLY, however, Colombia was in better economic shape than Venezuela, and the loss of Panama served as a jolt to draw the political factions together in a constitutional government that maintained peace and promoted progress through the first half of the 20th Century. These 50 years saw the expansion of smaller industries, the growth of the cities, the development of a national network of air transport, the building of railroads, highways and ports, and a major improvement in public health leading to a rapid increase in population.

Nevertheless, several factors persisted which distinguish Colombia's 20th Century economic progress from that of more developed nations. The secondary industries producing goods for local consumption depended on the big industrialized countries both for capital equipment and for a large part of the raw and semiprocessed materials they used. Imports had to be paid for by Colombia's traditional exports, and among these coffee continued to occupy a dominant place, accounting for about three quarters of all foreign exchange. But Colombia was not able to find a way to control the price of coffee and consequently never knew from one year to the next what foreign exchange might be available to pay for imports. Colombia was, however, unhappily aware of one basic economic fact: the trend of world markets was constantly widening the gap between the country's revenue and its needs. As developed nations progress, they spend proportionately less of their income on raw materials and on food. The suppliers of these products consequently are faced with a constantly shrinking share of world trade.

THE continuing control today of the distribution of the national income by Colombia's small group of wealthy people has also had a negative effect on the economy. The pay of workers and peasant farmers has remained so low that their purchasing power is marginal and industry therefore has not grown fast enough to absorb the steadily expanding labor force. This ultimately self-defeating refusal of the employers to pay a decent wage is long ingrained. Shortly before independence, in 1803, the Spanish Viceroy, Pedro Mendinueta, wrote a report concerning the landowners and businessmen of his day. The employers complain, he said, that the people are lazy, "but I have not heard of any rise in wages, and I understand that today [they] pay the same wage as 50 or more years ago, notwithstanding the rise in price of every necessity of life." Mendinueta went on to prophesy that "this is an injustice which cannot last long." On that point the Viceroy was wrong. The pattern of niggardly wages has not changed in more than a century and a half. Great masses of people, both in the cities and in the countryside, live at a subhuman level, constituting a drag on the economy and a threat to social stability.

During the first third of the 20th Century, Venezuela lagged behind Colombia in population and in development. Part of the problem, as it so often is in

South America, was the inordinate political power of the Army. While Colombia had succeeded in getting the Army out of its politics, Venezuela was groaning under the most arbitrary military dictatorship in its history. Yet it was a dictatorship which would be viewed in retrospect as having started the country toward a better future.

THE United States was responsible in part for launching the dictator, Juan Vicente Gómez, on his sordid way. His predecessor, the dictator Cipriano Castro, had built up a vast personal fortune but he had no intention of using it to help pay the country's foreign debts. Instead, he decided in 1908 to take a trip to Europe. Years of debauchery had left him in bad shape, and he wanted to consult a German kidney specialist.

Gómez, Castro's trusted lieutenant, had been waiting for just this moment. He got in touch with the U.S. State Department and persuaded its policy makers that he would pay the country's debts and in general be a better friend of the United States than Castro had been. American cruisers were sent to La Guaira to demonstrate in Gómez' favor, and a bloodless coup gave Venezuela a new ruler.

Venezuelans recall the "Age of Gómez" much as do Christians that of Nero in Rome. Gómez was born in 1857 to mestizo parents in a small Andean village. A virtually illiterate peasant, he won the favor of Cipriano Castro by recruiting an army of cowboys which helped Castro to seize the presidency. Tall, well built and muscular, Gómez was often called "The Catfish" because of his bushy mustache, slanted eyes and heavy eyelids. He looked so much like Joseph Stalin in his later years that the theory has been advanced that he fathered Stalin by a Russian ballerina who visited Colombia. He had Stalin's peasant cunning to such a degree that Venezuelans also called him "The Sorcerer" and credited him with the ability to read people's minds. The Venezuelans became so accustomed to his tricks that they refused to believe the announcement of his death in 1935. When, after several days, they finally became convinced that the news was true, they danced in the streets to celebrate their freedom.

Freedom was in short supply during the Age of Gómez. Fortunately for Gómez, money was not.

What made his life easy was the discovery of vast quantities of petroleum. Gómez sold concessions to U.S. and European oil companies for what—for Venezuela—were large sums of money. In retrospect it appears that the oil companies got much the best of these deals. Between 1922 and 1936 the Venezuelan treasury received only from 7 to 10 per cent in royalties on all the oil extracted from Venezuelan soil. But since Venezuela did not have the capital or the equipment to drill for the oil, Gómez was forced to make the best bargains he could with outsiders. In any case, the oil revenues enabled Gómez to keep his pledge to finish paying off the foreign debt— and to line his pockets and those of his favorites.

The long-term effects on Venezuela of Gómez's fiscal policies, however, were unfortunate. The sudden availability of unlimited foreign exchange caused an economic deformation which ruined the countryside. Landowners, realizing they could make more money channeling their capital into the expanding urban sector of the economy, did nothing to improve their farms. The production of coffee and other export crops fell off. Worse, with agriculture depressed, there were fewer jobs for a constantly expanding population. Rural workers flocked to the oil fields and the cities in search of employment, but again there were fewer jobs than there were men. While the rich were rapidly growing richer, the gap between them and the majority was constantly widening.

A LEADING cause of this dangerous gap between the few haves and the many have-nots, which is equally serious in both Colombia and Venezuela, is the persistence of the *mantuano* mentality so perceptively defined by Alexander von Humboldt. If the rich no longer insist on the exclusive right to wear capes and silk and lace, they still do begrudge a fair share in their nations' wealth to the "inferior castes." And they have often seemed perversely determined to hold onto their privileges even at the risk of having the entire fabric of their societies rent asunder by the explosive force of revolution. The *llaneros*, the rugged horsemen of the plains, whose discontent fueled the War for Independence, are no longer a force. But their descendants, living in impoverished rural areas or in hideous urban slums, may prove as volatile and hard to control.

Influential Colombian businessman Alvaro Caicedo (at right) discusses expansion with top executives of his family's companies.

Redirecting the Uses of Great Wealth and Power

Some of the leading industrialists in Colombia and Venezuela are beginning to rethink old notions about the economic structure of their region. Traditionally the ownership class secreted its wealth and took little interest in the people. But this is beginning to change as businessmen perceive that the vast gulf between the wealthy few and the impoverished many is creating a situation that could lead to violent upheavals. Among the businessmen taking an enlightened attitude is Colombia's Alvaro Caicedo (*above and pages 76-77*), whose family's companies

began social benefits for their workers before the catalytic 1959 Cuban revolution and recently increased them. He even started a newspaper to make contact with "the common people." Another progressive businessman is Venezuela's Eugenio Mendoza (*pages 78-79*). Long interested in philanthropy but hardly a radical reformer, Mendoza now backs the Alliance for Progress, the U.S. program that has made social reform a condition for aid. The political fates of Colombia and Venezuela may well depend on how many others follow the lead of such men.

EXAMINING MACHINERY, Alvaro Caicedo talks with a worker at one of his sugar mills in the Andean city of Cali. The large mill annually turns out 65,000 tons of sugar.

INSPECTING A PLANT, Caicedo marches across a courtyard with three managers *(right)*. Caicedo Enterprises also owns cane fields, a cattle ranch, a candy factory and a newspaper.

VISITING THE SICK in a hospital maintained by his sugar mill for its employees *(below)*, Caicedo chats with a cane-field worker. Medical care for the Caicedo workers is free.

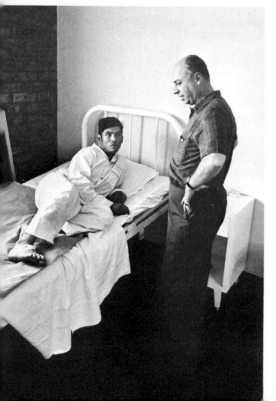

ATTENDING THE SENATE in Bogotá, Caicedo exchanges words with some employees of the Senate office building. As a Senator he tries to reconcile unions and management.

EDITING HIS PAPER, Caicedo examines an edition of *Occidente (below)*, a journal he founded in Cali to interpret capitalism to labor. Caicedo is part owner of six radio stations.

ENERGETIC BUSINESSMAN, wealthy Alvaro Caicedo seeks to improve Colombia's economy and aid the worker

RELAXING AT HOME, Caicedo shares a joke with his two young sons and his wife in the patio of their mansion in Cali. The family descends from Spanish conquistadors. Caicedo conceives of his role as businessman-politician-publisher as a hereditary responsibility.

ON HIS ESTATE, Eugenio Mendoza, one of Venezuela's major industrialists, rides a horse down a lane of trees. His business empire includes construction, lumber and dairy concerns.

IN A BOARD MEETING, Mendoza commands the rapt attention of the directors of his Mendoza Group companies (below). Many of the company's plants are pictured on the wall.

A LEADING CAPITALIST, Venezuela's Eugenio Mendoza is a generous philanthropist

AT HIS ENDOWED SCHOOL, Mendoza passes under a banner with the institution's name, "Faith and Happiness." He built the school in memory of his late son, also named on the banner.

AT A PUBLIC HOSPITAL that he helps support, Mendoza walks with a young polio victim *(left)*. Mendoza's other philanthropies include scholarships and many cultural projects.

A MODERN HOME accommodates José Paolini, 30, his wife and their proud possession, a new U.S.-made car *(above)*. The comfortable house is near the Lake Maracaibo oil wells, where José is a construction supervisor.

A SKILLED CREW gets its instructions from Paolini *(left)* on a barge used for his specialty, the construction of oil flow stations. The stations perform the function of separating oil and natural gas.

TOWERING OIL DERRICKS that rise out of Lake Maracaibo *(opposite)* belong to Paolini's employers, the Creole Petroleum Corporation. Paolini came to the area from the Venezuelan plains.

A CAREFUL INSPECTOR, Paolini checks the gauges and machinery *(below)* used in extracting oil from the sands beneath the lake. About 75 per cent of Venezuela's oil comes from the Lake Maracaibo region.

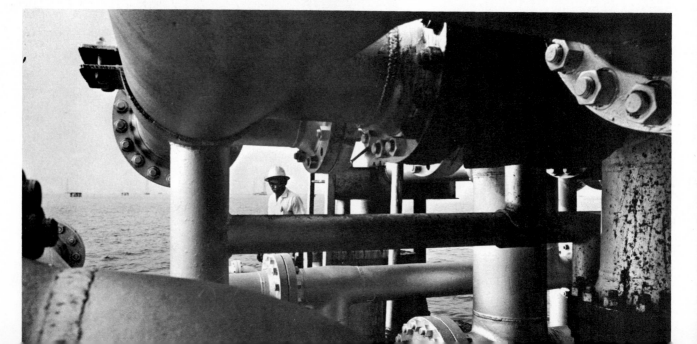

VENEZUELAN OIL brings prosperity to middle-class technicians such as José Paolini

A BUSY HELICOPTER lifts a motor into the dense rain forest near the Ecuadorian border. The region's oil reserves have been known for years, but the torrential rains have frustrated all efforts to build roads into the area.

A CAPPED WELL stands ready for use *(left)*. The Texas Petroleum Company is planning to open a pipeline to connect such wells to the coast. Then these new oil fields will be of immense value to the Colombian economy.

SECTIONS OF PIPE are lowered from a helicopter at a well in the process of being sunk *(right)*. Some roads link the completed wells, but the region can be reached from outside only by helicopter or by long canoe trips.

FIELD GEOLOGISTS, forming the advance guard of the oil-drilling operation, camp at a remote jungle station *(below)*. After they arrived, a tractor, airlifted piece by piece, was used to clear the space for their tents.

6

Colombia's Uncertain Present

FEW sights match a flight of scarlet ibis seen against a sunset as they rise from the waters of the Orinoco. The flame-colored wings slowly, majestically lift the glistening bodies, heavy with fish, from the waters of the river.

The ibis delights the eye. It is, however, not nearly as clever as a bird called the hoatzin. This strange creature shares with the ibis the same nesting places in the deep jungles on the borders of Colombia and Venezuela, and both birds hatch their young in thorn trees when the rains flood the plains. If an ibis chick, frightened by some intruder, falls off its thorn-tree branch into the water, a shoal of deadly piranha fish quickly picks its bones. Not so the baby hoatzin. At a sign of danger, the chick drops into the water where, protected by its piranha-repellent odor, it lies submerged until the enemy moves on. Then it uses the unique claws which are attached to its wings to climb back up the tree into its nest.

Colombia's ruling class is like the hoatzin. It does not fight the challenger. When its security is threatened, it drops out of sight. But it has mysterious powers of self-preservation. With disarming sophistication, it yields on the visible level, while holding on below the surface to the reality of control. Unlike less enlightened ruling classes in a number of other South American countries, Colombia's has never resisted economic development. It is satisfied that it can regulate the changes within the power structure, determine their scope and character, and emerge always in possession.

Whether Colombia's ruling class can continue to control the country is, however, becoming steadily more open to question. The needs of an industrial society, and the independent attitudes it fosters, are ultimately incompatible with paternalistic rule by a small oligarchy. The substantial progress Colombia's leaders have made in modernizing the country's economy is, in fact, the surest guarantee that their efforts to hold back political and social change will fail. Agricultural workers on isolated estates are far easier to rule than industrial workers living in cities, and the great increase in the number of white-collar workers—the rise of a bourgeoisie—has signaled the doom of aristocracies throughout modern history. The mounting class tensions which plague Colombia are in part a result of progress battling outmoded social stratifications.

ECONOMIC progress in Colombia has in fact been remarkable during this century. Of incalculable benefit was the advent of the airplane, permitting for the first time quick and easy travel among the scattered parts of the country. Colombia had the first regularly scheduled airline on either of the American continents in 1919. This early air service quickly expanded and before long formed a network of national dimensions. Still more important was the formation during the 1920s of a federation of coffeegrowers. This federation has since played an important part in Colombia's national life and the coffee its members have produced has been the foundation of the country's mercantile progress. The federation set quality controls for exports and established Colombian coffee as one of the world's best. Facilities were created to stockpile millions of bags of coffee in periods of surplus so that the price would not tumble. A network of research stations improved coffee strains and modernized the industry. Colombia also took the lead in promoting cooperation among all the coffee-producing countries, sponsoring international agreements which it was hoped would cushion the price swings which unfortunately characterize the world market in coffee, as in other agricultural commodities.

Since coffee gave Colombia considerable cash income, the country became an attractive market for manufactured goods. Colombia's own city of Medellín early established small-scale industries, but the market for goods was mostly supplied by Europe and the United States until World War II. The shortages that then developed gave a great impetus to Colombia's industrial expansion, particularly in the processing of foodstuffs and the manufacture of textiles. The food industry is characterized by a number of medium to large companies, while textiles are dominated by a few giants. The Coltejer textile company has eight plants in and around the city of Medellín and employs some 10,000 workers, more than any other single company in Colombia. Fabricato, in the nearby town of Bello, is also large, employing 6,200 workers.

To a degree exceptional in Latin America, Colombia's manufacturing industries were started by Colombians, and continue to be owned and managed by them. Many of these businessmen have come from the Antioquia region. The enterprising Basque settlers of Antioquia possess the practical, capitalist sense characteristic of the English and North Americans rather than the princely attitudes of the Spaniards. Seizing an opportunity, they expanded coffee production in the late 19th Century and the early 20th to keep pace with a rapidly growing world demand, and it was they who used the profits from coffee to make Medellín the manufacturing center it is today.

THE Antioquians are enterprising, but, like the other segments of Colombia's ruling class, they are also very conservative. They try to retain in industry the paternalistic relationship with the workers which was traditional between landowners and their peons. Even the most modern plants reflect this outlook. Wages are low, but the workers receive a number of "fringe benefits" in facilities operated by the employers. Such benefits include cafeterias serving inexpensive meals, clinics, subsidized housing, swimming pools and workers' clubs.

Despite their paternalistic conservatism, Colombia's businessmen would have industrialized the country even faster than they have but for a shortage of capital to build new plants. This shortage of growth capital can be traced back to difficulties in the country's vital coffee export trade which even the coffeegrowers' federation has not been able to solve. World coffee production in the recent decades has outstripped the world's ability to consume it. As a result Colombia cannot always sell all the coffee it grows, and coffee prices, even for the excellent Colombian beans, have been low.

FLOWING into this vacuum has come a considerable amount of foreign investment, principally from the United States. Subsidiaries of U.S. and European firms are now involved in such businesses as automobile assembly and the manufacture of drugs, rubber goods and chemicals. The United States is heavily represented in oil production and refining. The petroleum industry is much less important in Colombia than it is in Venezuela, but Colombia's oil fields and refineries still supply almost all of the country's domestic needs, and petroleum products are the second most important export commodity after coffee. An important new oil deposit was found by a United States company in 1963 in a remote jungle area near the Ecuadorian border, and the impact on the economy should be significant when pipelines across the Andes begin to carry the oil to the coast. Meanwhile, at Cartagena, another United States oil company has opened one of the world's biggest ammonia and nitric-acid plants, raising hope of a major petrochemical industry.

This period of vigorous industrial growth since World War II has brought in its wake severe social pressures and unrest of a kind not previously known in Colombia. The primary reason undoubtedly has been the rapid rise in population without a corresponding increase in living resources for the masses. Industrial expansion has helped to relieve some of the pressure by providing jobs. In another respect, however, industrialization has accentuated the trouble. Labor unions have formulated the demands of the urban workers and challenged the claim of the employers to be the sole judges of what is good for the country. Class issues consequently have been defined more sharply than ever before.

But the main source of trouble has been the 20th Century's population explosion, which has proved particularly acute in Colombia. The country had fewer than four million people in 1900, but by 1950 there were 11 million and estimates project a staggering rise to 20 million by 1970. It is true that density of population in relation to territory is still low, but density in relation to actual economic opportunity is tragically high in some parts of the country. This situation is particularly marked in the coffee-growing valleys of the Andes. The rich, flat land of the valley bottoms is still controlled by wealthy landowners whose big estates produce sugar cane, cotton and cattle. The slopes of the mountains where the coffee is grown, however, have been so divided and subdivided to accommodate the burgeoning population that many of the peasant coffeegrowers can no longer make a living from their tiny holdings.

IT is precisely these increasingly overpopulated coffee regions that have experienced the main impact of an extraordinary and horrible social disease known to Colombians as *la violencia*. This is a special kind of violence which for more than a generation has been driving Colombians to kill each other, savagely and purposelessly. It has taken many forms. At times it expresses itself as a clash between groups calling themselves Liberals and Conservatives, at times as anti-state activities instigated by Castroites or Communists, at times as old-fashioned barbarity.

La violencia is fed by the sons of farmers. Faced with the prospect of having to leave the tiny family plot and struggle for a job among the unemployed in the cities, many prefer to go back into the depths of the mountains and enlist in bands of desperadoes. They do not hope to achieve anything significant by their rebellion. At most, they may win a brief moment of local glory before falling to the bullets of troops sent to hunt them down. Their activities are characterized by pathological barbarity. A group of bandits occupies a village or an isolated homestead, or it ambushes a bus, and then the bandits slaughter every man, woman and child, mutilating bodies and chopping off heads with cutlasses.

The origins of *la violencia* go back to the 1930s Depression, but it did not assume major proportions until 1948. What sparked it then was the assassination of a popular politician named Jorge Gaitán. Gaitán had come into prominence some years earlier as a potential leader of the previously unrepresented masses. Ambitious and opinionated, he was also sincerely concerned about rural and urban misery, convinced that the oligarchy's control over society must end. The oligarchy for its part closed ranks against him. Even the leaders of Gaitán's own Liberal Party feared his views were too radical and opposed him when he ran for the presidency in 1946, preferring to let the Conservative candidate win. But Gaitán retained the confidence of the masses and continued an unceasing though fruitless agitation in Congress on behalf of the workers.

The circumstances surrounding his killing on a Bogotá street are confused. Onlookers immediately seized the assassin and beat him to death on the spot. Before they had finished their task, a large mob had gathered. Long pent-up resentments were suddenly released, revealing the intensity of the people's discontent. For days, the mob swept the city in a senseless outburst of pillage, looting and burning that gave the Spanish language a new word, a *bogotazo*. From the capital the riots spread across the country, causing damage estimated by the United States Embassy at more than half a billion dollars. Professor John D. Martz has summed up the views of political analysts and historians. "The *bogotazo* was more than a dramatic outpouring of emotion and unrestrained, bestial violence. With the veneer of civilization stripped away, the entire moral fabric of the nation was revealed in its rotting reality. The people were demanding a social revolution in brutal terms."

THE people were demanding, but Colombia's ruling class was still unwilling to effect any major reforms. They called out the Army to try to restore order, but, with their customary sophistication, they did not attempt a direct challenge while passions were inflamed, preferring to experiment with a conciliatory approach. A series of Government decrees sought to improve the people's living conditions. These decrees included a land distribution measure described as necessary "to bring about social stability by increasing the number of proprietors." Both the Liberal and Conservative parties rallied behind President Mariano Ospina Pérez in a Government of National Union. Tension eventually relaxed, and 251 days after Gaitán's assassination the emergency was officially declared at an end.

As the immediate danger passed, however, the wealthy lost their enthusiasm for sacrifice. Pressures grew to substitute repression for conciliation, a policy which was formalized by the arch-conservative Laureano Gómez when he replaced Ospina Pérez as president in 1950. It did not take the new President long to undo whatever good had been accomplished by the Government of National Union. A member of the Conservative Party's reactionary Right Wing, Laureano Gómez had been for many years the party's most powerful leader. Before World War II he had been openly pro-German and later he continued to proclaim the virtues of Franco Spain as an example for Colombia. Wealthy, aggressive and violent, he took advice only from himself.

THE Liberal Party, representing the progressive and mildly anticlerical segment of Colombia's upper class, had opposed the Laureano Gómez candidacy. Soon it was joined in opposition by the moderates among the Conservatives. Gómez replied by launching the military police on a program of savage persecution of all his enemies throughout the country. Instead of pacification, however, all Gómez achieved was an intensification of *la violencia*. There was universal relief, accordingly, when the Army abandoned its long tradition of political neutrality, deposed Gómez and substituted General Gustavo Rojas Pinilla as president in 1953.

But it was not easy to undo the evil wrought by Gómez. Although the tempo of *la violencia* soon declined, the disease had become endemic. An estimated 100,000 had been killed during the five years between the assassination of Gaitán and the deposition of Laureano Gómez in 1953. Although figures vary, it is estimated that at least another 100,000 have died in the years since Gómez was deposed.

The joy of the politicians at the change of regime did not last long. Assuming the mantle of the slain Gaitán and proclaiming himself the enemy of the existing order, Rojas Pinilla set out to establish broad popular support among the industrial workers and even to create a movement similar to that of the *descamisados*, the "shirtless ones," which flourished during the years of Juan Perón's rule in Argentina. Popular approval was immediate, and *la violencia* declined significantly in a few months. But, just as quickly, the two traditional parties closed ranks against Rojas Pinilla, and he resorted to tyranny to preserve his power. The Church denounced him, and the Army withdrew its support, permitting his ouster in a bloodless coup in 1957.

The man who engineered the coup is a rarity among Colombian politicians, a man who puts the nation above party or sectional interest. Alberto Lleras Camargo is modern Colombia's most brilliant statesman. He was Colombia's delegate to the San Francisco Conference in 1945 which drew up the United Nations charter. Later in that same year he was named interim president of Colombia. When his term expired in 1946 he went to Washington for eight years as Director General of the Pan American Union and later first Secretary General of the Organization of American States. Combining a talent for compromise with a regard for principle, he is respected by all segments of Colombian national opinion. When he became president in 1958 even those who did not share his liberal views liked the moderation with which he promoted them. To avoid chaos they were willing to accept his leadership.

The formula for peace and progress drawn up by Lleras Camargo was founded on a proposal that there be a 16-year political truce. Liberals and Conservatives would be represented equally in the executive, legislative and judiciary branches of the Government and in the diplomatic service. The presidency would alternate between the two parties every four years. The proclaimed purpose of Lleras Camargo's plan was to develop the economy and carry through major social reforms within the constitutional framework. But the formula contained a basic flaw—it left political power undisturbed in the hands of the traditional politicians. They could still control, as they always had, the rate, scope and character of change. Even during the years from 1958 to 1962

COLOMBIA'S BUCCANEER ISLANDS

On two charming little Colombian islands the memory of the buccaneer era of three centuries ago lingers on. The 5,000 inhabitants of San Andrés and Providencia—located 400 miles northwest of Cartagena—speak the English language first introduced into the islands by British Puritans. The Puritans arrived 90 strong in 1631 after hearing reports of the agricultural fertility of the islands. They did not restrict themselves to farming, however, and their stern, Puritanical principles did not last long in the balmy Caribbean. Within a few years they brought in slaves to do their work and began raiding Spanish gold shipments. Eventually they were dispersed by the Spaniards, but later the islands became a base for other pirates. Today their English-speaking offspring live by the comparatively prosaic occupations of farming, fishing and serving tourists.

while Lleras Camargo himself was President it became evident that the virtues of his plan were more negative than positive. The powerful forces opposed to social change reduced the Congress almost to stagnancy. It took two years to achieve agreement on the terms of a land reform measure although it had been understood from the outset that the most urgent task facing the coalition was far-reaching agrarian reform. Once passed, the measure was immediately challenged in the courts and it took another year for a final ruling on its constitutionality. Another defect of the political truce had also come to light before Lleras Camargo's term ended. Since each party automatically gets half of the seats in Congress, elections amount to little more than jockeying for position within the party. It is as if elections in the United States consisted only of the primaries. Colombia's elections have become relatively peaceful, but they have failed to produce new, vital leaders who might come to the surface in the rough-and-tumble of real political contests.

In addition, Lleras Camargo's formula provided that a two-thirds vote was necessary to pass any legislation. Since the Congress is equally divided between the two parties, this means in practice that the Government cannot win Congressional approval of any strong action. Even the choice of a president to succeed Lleras Camargo was determined by this fact. Guillermo León Valencia, selected in 1962, was acceptable to all not only because he was a Conservative but also because he was irresolute. In office, he has not disappointed his selectors in this respect.

La violencia had declined in the first years of the Rojas Pinilla dictatorship, but it spread once more when that regime degenerated into tyranny. The creation of Lleras Camargo's National Front reduced tensions between Liberals and Conservatives in the country and this again was quickly reflected in a lowering of the number of violent deaths. But *la violencia* was far from over. On the contrary, banditry during the early 1960s began to develop its own institutions. Successful outlaws set themselves up as war lords in control of substantial areas of the country. The most important autonomous area was the self-styled "independent republic" of Marquetalia in the departments of Tolima and Huila. This mountain fastness had been occupied 10 years earlier, in 1952, by Liberal guerrillas fleeing the attacks of their Conservative neighbors who were riding high under the Laureano Gómez regime. Bandit groups based in this area roamed the countryside, taxing the peasants. Similar bandit nests came into being at Sumapaz, Río Chiquito, Guayabero and El Pato.

ALL through the 1950s the Army had made a major effort to destroy the bandits and their strongholds. The effort was intensified, with considerable United States help, after Castro's rise to power in Cuba fomented unrest all over Latin America, particularly in Colombia and Venezuela. *La violencia* then took on an ideological hue. For a time it threatened to become a nationwide guerrilla war, supported by trained Communists and fed with outside arms and supplies.

The military countermeasures long met with indifferent success. The Army could concentrate enough force to take any selected objective. But the guerrillas melted into the mountains, to return when the soldiers moved on to their next task. Finally, however, a high officer, General Alberto Ruiz Novoa, hit on a technique which produced spectacular results. He followed up each military action with a rehabilitation campaign. Strict control of the soldiers protected the civil liberties of the peasants even during hostilities. When order was established, a survey of local needs was conducted. Public works projects were started and help given for community development and the improvement of public health facilities.

Inauguration of the land reform program also helped to lessen rural tensions. An Institute of Agrarian Reform was set up in 1962, and it moved quickly to appropriate several thousand acres of land which had been left unused by their owners for 10 or more years. By the end of 1964 it had settled 20,000 peasant families on farms large enough to be worked efficiently, and it promised to settle a further 30,000 during 1965.

The combined effect of all these measures was to make life in the countryside much safer during 1964. The number of violent deaths declined significantly. In addition, the Army captured many of the leading bandits and forced others to withdraw far from populated areas. But public satisfaction at this progress was tempered by a new wave of terrorism in the cities. During one week, more than 20 bombs exploded in Bogotá, including one thrown at the home of ex-dictator Laureano Gómez. Several prisons were attacked. Police investigating an explosion which destroyed a house near Bogotá found nearby a large amount of dynamite, other materials for making bombs, and large quantities of Communist propaganda.

The urban dissatisfaction which the Communists were exploiting had solid foundations. A devaluation of the peso in late 1962 and other factors had produced a 50 per cent rise in the cost of living in two years. President León Valencia did not help the emotional situation when he denounced demands of the workers for wage readjustments as "a sophism of international Communism designed to produce the financial collapse of the Republic." To add to the confusion, the department of education had severe budget trouble and was unable to meet even current teacher salaries. This provoked widespread strikes of both primary and secondary teachers.

THE hungry people took a new look at the National Front. In the March 1964 elections for Congress, two thirds of the voters registered their disillusionment by staying at home. Only 23 per cent of the people voted for National Front candidates. Opposition deputies grew from 39 to 56 in a House with 184 members. One of those most pleased with the election results was former dictator Rojas Pinilla. Not only had the people rejected the National Front, he claimed, but the fact that 27 of his followers had been elected showed that many of the people were looking to him to save them once more from the politicians.

Another serious threat appeared almost simultaneously in the person of Ruiz Novoa, the general and War Minister whose success in dealing with rural banditry had won universal acclaim. Riding on his popularity, he began to call for more basic social reforms than the oligarchy-dominated Congress was willing to grant. Poverty, he told the press, is not to blame for Colombia's backwardness. At fault are archaic social structures, an unjust land tenure system in which farms are either too big or too small, low wages and too many pressure groups blocking reform.

A SCORE of voices was raised against Ruiz Novoa for talking politics while he was War Minister. Others defended him, including an influential bureaucrat with liberal leanings named Enrique Peñalosa, the head of Colombia's land reform institute. Early in 1965, however, the Ruiz Novoa threat aborted. Ruiz Novoa had long ignored President León Valencia's instructions to stay out of politics while on active service and many believed that he was simply waiting for the right moment to seize power. For once, the usually indecisive León Valencia took a firm stand. He fired Ruiz Novoa from his job as War Minister.

For several days the country held its breath, waiting for the Army's reaction. Soon, however, rumors that the Army chiefs had spurred the presidential action were confirmed. Ruiz Novoa resigned his commission and withdrew to private life. It was clear that he lacked the means to maneuver a coup, even if he had sought to do so. It was equally clear that he had no future as a constitutional politician.

But if the potential perils of having a popular military man invade public life were avoided, at least for the time being, a number of other difficulties remained and grew more pressing. The country's cost of living was spiraling upward. The foreign debt had doubled since President León Valencia took office and had reached $750 million—an amount more than sufficient to alarm foreign creditors. An epidemic of kidnapings by terrorists frightened both the city and the countryside.

Worst of all, the National Front itself appeared to be in danger of collapse. The governmental arrangements which had worked, after a fashion, during the presidency of the highly respected Lleras Camargo seemed totally incapable of responding to any crisis under President León Valencia. Instead of laws they

spawned an unwieldy bureaucracy. Instead of issuing bold statements of principle, León Valencia merely reiterated his determination, come what may, to finish out his term.

The most serious crisis loomed as the time came to choose the next president. Since León Valencia was a Conservative, the new man, in accord with the rules of the National Front, had to be a Liberal. The candidate proposed by the National Front for the 1966 election was Carlos Lleras Restrepo, a longtime Liberal firebrand who had made many enemies and who was anathema to the whole Conservative sector of the ruling class. The National Front, which was supposed, as its name implies, to be based on quiet cooperation, exploded in angry controversy. Into this confusion stepped ex-dictator Rojas Pinilla to head an anti-Front coalition which picked up strength from a splinter faction of León Valencia's own Conservative Party and some dissident Liberals. Rojas Pinilla vowed that "In congressional elections next March we will get enough votes to void the National Front and move right into the Presidential Palace." Despite the fact that he controlled no press or radio facilities which could spread his oratory to the mass of the people, Rojas Pinilla seemed to be getting his message across.

T HE basic, underlying flaw, which had all but paralyzed Colombia's democratic processes and had brought onto the scene terrorists, military men and ex-dictators, was the stubborn refusal of the ruling class, the oligarchy, to surrender its control. The forms of democracy were there, but the people who really ran the National Front were members of the same old families of affluence and power. Like the hoatzin bird they had proved uncannily adept at self-preservation, whatever the threat. But evidence was mounting that their grip on the reins of government, sooner or later, would have to give way.

To create opportunity for the vast and growing numbers of unproductive Colombians required a sense of purpose which was little evident among these rulers. The continuing and growing crisis also called for the mobilization of all the nation's resources. And that could not really begin until the people of wealth and power—the oligarchy—became willing to abandon their privileged position.

A Closed Society's Charm and Despair

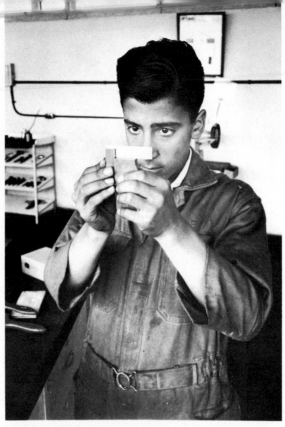

A VOCATIONAL STUDENT, Henry Junca, 15, learns how to measure an angle in a school in Bogotá. Although Colombia has trained some skilled workers it lacks primary schools.

Colombia has an impressive history, vast potential wealth and pervasive Old World charm. Unlike many of its neighbors it has had long periods of political stability. The limited democracy it has enjoyed for half a century has resisted equally the encroachments of revolutionaries and of militarist dictators. Yet to a majority of Colombia's people, this stability has meant only that the dominant facts of life have continued to be poverty, illiteracy and disease. The isolation caused by rugged terrain and the economic concentration resulting from reliance on a single crop, coffee, have tended to reinforce the power of the small group of wealthy men who have traditionally run the country. And although the resulting closed society has been the basis for a measure of tranquillity, it has also been the cause of a wave of senseless violence born of poverty and frustration.

A BIRTH-CONTROL CLASS, limited to giving out only information approved by the Roman Catholic Church, is conducted by a doctor near Cali. Most of the participants are illiterate.

A GAUDY PARADE surges down the main street of Manizales (*opposite*) to celebrate a coffee festival. Manizales is an important commercial city in the coffee-growing province of Caldas.

SHADOWY CHAPEL off the central nave of the Church of San Francisco in Popayán is lit by a single window. The baroque carving on the chairs is characteristic of Spanish artwork.

A SUNLIT PATIO surrounded by balconies *(below)* lies at the center of the monastery of La Santa Cruz in Cartagena, an ancient port city founded in 1533 by Spanish conquistadors.

The wind-swept fort of San Felipe stands within the walls of Cartagena. Begun

and fortifications of Colombian cities a timeless air

in 1634 and finished in 1735, the city's walls average 40 feet high and 55 feet thick

A DARK DOORWAY frames a profusion of flowers at San Pedro Claver monastery in Cartagena *(above)*. The monastery was built in 1603 and later dedicated to a saint who aided slaves.

A TREASURED BELL that rang in commemoration of Cartagena's independence from Spain in 1811 hangs in the Church of San Pedro Claver *(below)*. Simón Bolívar used the city as a base.

THE NATION'S NERVE CENTER, downtown Bogotá's shining office buildings house the banks and businesses controlled by Colombia's entrenched well-to-do. Political as well as economic power is concentrated in Bogotá since it is the nation's capital and, under Colombia's centralized form of government, controls all important provincial administrations.

A FORMER DICTATOR, General Gustavo Rojas Pinilla, ousted in 1957, goes on trial in 1959 *(above)* for abuse of power. Five years later he won 18 per cent of the Presidential vote.

A POLITICAL ARCHITECT, Alberto Lleras Camargo *(left)* greets well-wishers at the dedication of a railroad. He planned the system by which Colombia's two parties share power.

A TROUBLED PRESIDENT, Guillermo León Valencia *(below)*, elected in 1962, has shown concern over his nation's economic situation. The economy slowed down after he came to office.

BLOODY UPHEAVALS, known as "la violencia," shatter the peace of Colombian life

RAMPAGING RIOTERS, participants in the 1948 mob violence that wrecked sections of Bogotá, burn streetcars in the heart of the city. The *bogotazo*, as it has been called, started when a popular Liberal politician named Jorge Gaitán was murdered in a Bogotá street. In the rioting, looting and vandalism that followed, several thousand people were killed. In ensuing years, disorders, collectively known as *la violencia*—sometimes a matter of politics and sometimes of simple banditry—claimed an estimated 200,000 lives.

98

A BODY-LITTERED STREET testifies to the bitterness with which authorities put down a student demonstration in 1954. The trouble began when soldiers opened fire on a group of young people who were returning from a memorial service held for a student martyr.

AN ANTIGUERRILLA BATTALION enters the recently abandoned headquarters *(above)* of a famous bandit, Pedro Antonio Marín, known as *Tiro Fijo* ("Sure Shot"). Marín had directed his men in a campaign of terror and extortion in the upper Magdalena River valley.

A DEAD POLICEMAN, a recent victim of *la violencia*, is carried through the main street of the little town of Simacota *(right)*, located near Bucaramanga in the northeastern part of Colombia. The policeman was killed in a fight against bandits in January of 1965.

The Venezuelan Chamber of Deputies takes up Government measures. Venezuela's legislative branch, more representative than that of most

Latin American countries, has on occasion challenged the executive.

7

Trial and Triumph in Venezuela

A VITAL activity of the bootlickers and public relations operators who surround Latin American strongmen is to dream up distinguishing titles. Juan Vicente Gómez, Venezuela's dictator from 1908 to 1935, was the Well-Deserving, the Restorer and the Hero of Peace and Work.

The crowds which danced deliriously in the streets to celebrate Gómez's death plainly believed that the old dictator had not deserved such honorifics. In fact, they were in no mood to give him credit for having done anything constructive. Nevertheless, Gómez's 27-year tyranny produced two developments which enabled Venezuela to enter the modern world. It downgraded the power of the landowners, ending their control of public affairs, and it broke the hold of the country's regional bosses.

One of Venezuela's great weaknesses in the 19th Century was an almost total absence of respect for the national Government. Each province had its local leaders able and ready to raise an army and sell it to the politician who offered the province in return a license to despoil its neighbors. Gómez grew up under this system and he understood it. He set out during his first years in power to make binding agreements with the most important of the local chiefs. Later, however, he decided this would not work and he created a machinery of despotism which destroyed them utterly.

The kernel of Gómez's tyranny was an army and police force completely under the dictator's control. Their method was, simply, terror—dungeons, torture and an exemplary punishment for every offense, including any statement that might be interpreted as challenging the tyrant's wisdom or power. In the words of the Venezuelan historian Ramón Díaz Sánchez, Gómez made the country a "region par excellence of order and silence, a walled island completely surrounded by petroleum, without opinions, without feelings, without a window on the future."

GOMEZ was hard, cold and systematic. He regarded the country as his estate, and he ran it like a tyrannical landowner. Whoever wanted something had to come and search him out, wherever he might happen to be. He did not set up an efficient centralized administration in Caracas. On the contrary, government was by whim and intuition, not by plan. But Gómez did destroy political machinery and initiative outside Caracas and, as a by-product of his despotism, he converted Venezuela into a truly centralist state, even though the forms of a federation survived. After his death a monopoly of power in the capital became inevitable.

By concentrating decision-making power in his own hands, Gómez lessened the power of the landowners, a class already weakened by a century of civil wars. The death sentence of the old, landed ruling class, however, came from a different cause, the meteoric rise of the petroleum industry. Oil brought Venezuela previously unheard-of amounts of money. Gómez, astute peasant though he was, failed to understand what oil would do to Venezuela. He was dazzled by the sudden wealth and his reaction was that of a prospector who makes a lucky strike. He scattered gold to the four winds, rewarding his cronies lavishly, especially the Army officers on whom his power rested. The rest of the country caught the fever. With so much gold, it seemed silly to work any more. Venezuela unthinkingly committed itself to a policy of importation, not only of manufactures but also of foodstuffs. There was no inducement to start new industries, still less to plow part of the wealth back into agriculture.

Thus Gómez unwittingly finished off the old landed ruling class by destroying the economic basis of its power. Since his time, agriculture has been the most depressed sector of Venezuela's economy. Governments that came to power after Gómez's fall have done much to expand industry, but the countryside has never recovered from agriculture's decline.

More disastrous than the economic distortion left by Gómez was the intellectual and moral vacuum. Himself almost illiterate, Gómez had a deep distrust of learning and he ignored the movement toward universal education which characterized all civilized countries in his lifetime. Even the university, which in Latin America usually manages to retain some independence under dictatorial regimes, was subjugated during his years in office. When the students struck in 1928 to protest the jailing of some of their companions, Gómez sent the strikers to work under guard on the roads. Some died in prison, many were held for years. Others were exiled, or exiled themselves.

AS a result, when Gómez died after 27 years of despotic rule, there were no able leaders with experience in running the country's affairs. In addition, there was a universal sense of apathy. Corruption was so rife in government and business that the people saw no hope of ever creating an honest regime. They accordingly reconciled themselves to the inevitable when Congress, underlining the fact that the Army was the real ruler of Venezuela, named a general, Eleazar López Contreras, as President and Minister of War.

López Contreras made a number of concessions to those who, on Gómez's death, had called for liberty. He threw the most hated members of the Gómez gang out of the country. He abolished the censorship, allowed the political exiles to return and authorized the formation of trade unions. But he soon found that dictatorship and freedom do not mix. While he never attempted the savage repressions which had been the Gómez trademark, he withdrew many of the concessions, suppressing the opposition political parties, expelling labor leaders and crushing strikes.

Credit must be given to López Contreras and to his handpicked successor, Colonel Isaías Medina Angarita, for one essential advance. They secured a new agreement from the international oil companies on vastly more favorable terms.

Two external factors had conspired in their favor. One was Mexico's expropriation of its foreign oil interests in 1938. The other was World War II. The loss of their valuable properties in Mexico, then one of the world's major producers, caused the oil companies to re-evaluate their policies. They came to the conclusion that, to avoid further expropriations, they would have to give a bigger share of the profits to the countries owning the raw material. When war broke out, the United States added its voice on the same side. It was anxious to ensure the flow of Venezuelan oil while supplies from other parts of the world were jeopardized by the Axis powers.

Venezuela's new and more favorable agreement was reached in 1943. It increased the country's income from both royalties and taxes and guaranteed Venezuela an amount equal to the profits of the companies. In return, Venezuela renewed all of the oil companies' concessions for a period of 40 years. Venezuela subsequently increased to two thirds its share of the profits and introduced a policy of giving no further concessions. Existing concessions are still honored, but when foreign companies discover new fields they receive only the right to manage and operate them; the fields remain Venezuelan property. The historic agreement, nevertheless, is that of 1943. It guaranteed the income needed to modernize the economy.

It was during the López Contreras regime that the phrase "to sow the oil" came into vogue. It

---

THE GIANT OIL FIRMS OF TODAY

The Venezuelan oil industry is dominated by two companies, both foreign-owned. The larger of the two is Creole Petroleum Corporation, which is controlled by Standard Oil of New Jersey. Creole pumps 40 per cent of all the oil extracted from Venezuela and provides 25 per cent of the Government's income. Aware of Venezuela's many social problems, Creole supports a foundation that helps build schools and train teachers and has founded an investment corporation that assists small businesses by stock purchases. The company also participates in a program that provides funds for a variety of social projects. The second-largest oil company is Compañia Shell de Venezuela, a member of the Royal Dutch Shell group. A remarkably progressive firm, Shell de Venezuela has taken many steps to avoid the resentment often focused on foreign companies. It has established a scholarship program and provides homes, community centers, parks, schools and numerous other facilities for its workers.

---

expressed the principle that oil revenues were a national asset and should be used to develop other businesses which would replace these revenues when the oil was exhausted. But the slogan was far from a reality in the 1930s. Oil revenues, instead of going into private pockets directly, as often happened in the time of Gómez, were paid into the national treasury. But the change was merely technical as long as the people had no voice in the Government. Both López Contreras and Medina Angarita used the revenue to reward the supporters of their dictatorial regimes, and their top men accumulated large personal fortunes. Little was done to remove the distortions already caused in the economy by the oil money. Each year these distortions were becoming more acute. The population was growing—from 2.4 million in 1900 to 3.8 million in 1941—and the tempo of growth was accelerating. But the petroleum industry absorbed only 2 per cent of the work force, and its labor needs remained static while the total work force grew. The dictators' attention was concentrated only on the apparently endless wealth flowing from the oil wells. These men believed that a few handfuls of money judiciously scattered here and there would silence all grumbling. But other Venezuelans were less sure. The students who had been exiled by Gómez had wandered through the countries of Europe and America. Now they were home with new ideas, including the extreme ideologies of the Right and Left —Fascism and Communism—which had found currency during the 1930s. With the fervor of the converted, they preached to their fellow countrymen the good news that each of them had accepted in his years in exile from the homeland.

The most famous of these prophets was Rómulo Betancourt, a student leader of the abortive revolt of 1928. He had subsequently come under Marxist influences and had helped found the Communist Party of Costa Rica. Though he later drew away from Communism, he still preached a solution which for that period in South America was far to the left. He urged dividing up the big estates and distributing the land among the peasants, state-sponsored social security programs, free speech and universal education.

Meanwhile, many other parties took shape. Two Communist groups emerged to the left of Betancourt. Slightly to his right was Jóvita Villalba, a former colleague as a student leader. Then there were Rafael Caldera's Christian Democrats, whose revolutionary program was not at first understood because their original support came largely from Roman Catholic circles.

By far the most significant, however, was Betancourt's party, *Acción Democrática*, which by 1945 had some 20,000 members. When Medina Angarita's term as president was nearing its end, he tried to choose as his successor a candidate acceptable to Betancourt and his now powerful political party. The man he chose was, unfortunately, neither strong enough nor liberal enough, and so Betancourt conspired with a group of young Army officers to seize power in a coup. The coup succeeded and the officers named Betancourt provisional president. For two years, 1945 to 1947, the junta which he headed ruled by decree.

UNLIKE so many of his predecessors, Betancourt did not let power smother his principles. He laid the groundwork for democratic elections by passing an electoral law providing for universal suffrage. A Constituent Assembly in 1946 decreed that the president should be elected directly by the people and not, as before, chosen by Congress. In 1947, elections took place and Betancourt's *Acción Democrática* party won comfortable majorities in both houses of Congress. Its candidate for president, Rómulo Gallegos, a distinguished novelist, was also elected.

Efforts to implement the new Government's program soon, however, ran into considerable opposition. Strong vested interests opposed a number of laws aimed at modernizing Venezuelan society. The Roman Catholic clergy opposed laws reforming education. A program to divide up the land predictably raised the temperature of the landed aristocracy. Laws raising wages and a succession of other pro-labor actions aroused the hostility of both urban and rural employers.

The pressure from these influential groups was so strong that, when the new Government had been in office only nine months, the same secret society within the Army that had brought Betancourt to power in 1945, the Patriotic Military Union, re-entered the picture. It sent President Gallegos an ultimatum, demanding, among other things, several cabinet posts for the Army and the exile of Betancourt. When Gallegos refused, the Army seized power once more, expelled Gallegos, Betancourt and other key members of the Government from the country, and named a three-man junta to rule.

IT was the start of what was to become the infamous Pérez Jiménez dictatorship. General Marcos Pérez Jiménez was one of the three members of the junta which inaugurated its rule in 1948 with a promise of a new election, a new constitution and a new congress. Two years later, when Pérez Jiménez emerged as unchallenged dictator following the mysterious assassination of one of his colleagues, it was clear that the promises were meaningless. From 1950 to 1958 the only law Venezuelans knew was the arbitrary will of this pudgy, stammering, gold-braided officer.

Pérez Jiménez came from Táchira, the state which had given Venezuela many of its dictators, including Gómez—and his regime was a revival of Gómez's. Opposition party leaders were jailed or exiled. A police and spy organization was created. Censorship was introduced. Labor union leaders were removed from their posts. The armed forces were wooed with high salaries, luxury clubs for officers and an aura of prestige.

The dictatorship pursued the policy of sowing the petroleum, that is to say, of utilizing the oil revenues to develop the economy. Gradually, however, the application of the policy changed. Enormous sums were devoted to a modernization of Caracas. The capital had been growing very rapidly, and because of its location in a narrow mountain valley, space for expansion was extremely limited. A network of arterial roads was developed to ease the traffic, spreading out from a modern center which had become filled with imposing skyscrapers. A superhighway was cut through the mountains to shorten travel time to the harbor and airport.

Plans for heavy industry were drawn up on the same lavish scale. They included a petrochemical complex which was envisaged as a logical complement to the petroleum industry. These plans, like those for Caracas, were not unreasonable in themselves. The primary defect was that they were unnecessarily grandiose. In addition, their execution was shot through with waste and graft, a throwback to the Gómez formula. Finally, they ignored the more urgent needs of the great numbers of urban and rural unemployed.

While the urban construction provided some jobs, it increased social unrest by drawing the workless from the country into the city. Pérez Jiménez built an apartment house development for 200,000 people in Caracas, and many smaller housing projects. The rate of inflow, nevertheless, continued at a higher rate than the housing supply. The new occupants could not get steady work, nor did they know how to live in modern apartments. They tried to adapt their new abodes to their traditional village ways, filling them with chickens, goats and other animals.

MEANWHILE, the dictator caused further unrest by bulldozing the slum shacks as soon as their occupants found apartments. This was laudable —except that subsequent emigrants to the city could then find no place to live, and having a shack, however flimsy, is better than sleeping outdoors. And for all Pérez Jiménez's efforts, a survey taken a year after his fall revealed that almost a quarter of the population of Caracas was still living in the slums that form a ring of misery around the city.

Pérez Jiménez worked hard. In spite of his megalomaniacal schemes, the country made considerable progress. But the people had tasted the wine of freedom under the previous regime. The flat beer of doles and handouts would never again reconcile them to slavery. Try as he might, the dictator could not bring back the Age of Gómez. The persecuted political parties and unions retained the allegiance

of many followers. The business and commercial classes joined to oppose state control of all economic activities. The peasants and the urban workers saw the constantly widening gap between wealth and poverty.

Even within the armed forces, all was not well. A small clique of the dictator's close collaborators from the state of Táchira controlled advancement, and the others were outraged because their careers were at the mercy of these favorites. The Air Force and Navy resented Army domination. A number of younger officers, including some trained in the United States, were sincerely convinced that democracy was better for themselves and their country than dictatorship.

THE opponents of the Pérez Jiménez regime received a grave setback in 1954 when the President of the United States, Dwight D. Eisenhower, bestowed the Legion of Merit on the Venezuelan dictator, together with a citation praising his activities "while president and even before becoming president." This expression of Washington's favor served as a warning that plotters could expect no sympathy from the U.S. State Department.

Three years later, however, the situation changed for the better. In May 1957, the Roman Catholic Church publicly denounced Pérez Jiménez. Archbishop Rafael Arias spoke out against the "subhuman" conditions under which most people lived. The action was the more significant because the Church in Venezuela in recent decades has avoided interfering in politics. For the dictator, it was the beginning of the end. The archbishop's statement not only stirred Venezuelans but also aroused world opinion which previously had tended to accept the version of events distributed in endless profusion by the regime's paid propagandists.

Sensitive to external reaction, Pérez Jiménez hit on a scheme that he hoped would restore the confidence of the outside world, but which instead backfired badly. Cancelling the elections that had been scheduled for the fall of 1957, he announced a plebiscite in which voters would approve his continuance as President. The results of the plebiscite were announced only two hours after the polls closed. The affirmative vote, he said, was 85 per cent, a statement that public opinion both inside and outside the country recognized for what it was, the last desperate throw of a loser. Leaders of the outlawed political parties had already met in secret and had agreed on a common program. Revolutionary groups in the armed services attempted a coup. It failed, but it frightened many of the dictator's supporters, and they persuaded him to dismiss the head of the political police and other unpopular officials. But the people were not satisfied. The political parties called a general strike which led to street fighting in Caracas and other cities. The Navy revolted, and various Army officers joined in. Pérez Jiménez resigned and fled the country.

A provisional Government representing the political parties and the armed forces was formed, pledged to hold elections quickly. The pledge was honored and Rómulo Betancourt was chosen President. His *Acción Democrática* party won a majority in Congress and formed a coalition Government with two other parties that had fought Pérez Jiménez. It was the historic moment for which the Venezuelan people had waited. It marked the inauguration of the democratic regime which still continues and which seems to affirm each passing year that the Venezuelans can govern themselves.

Few governments anywhere ever took office with so much prestige and goodwill, both domestic and international. The dictatorship of Pérez Jiménez seemed to have had a catalytic effect on the country. It made Venezuelans realize that dictators would never bring clean government, that progress was possible only if the people ruled themselves. The Venezuelans also realized, for the first time, their own power. They had finally taken the initiative in destroying a tyranny. The Army was no longer the only force in the nation. If it had moved, it had moved in response to the people's expressed will.

THE FATE OF PEREZ JIMENEZ

Unlike most dictators who abscond from Latin American countries, Venezuela's former President Marcos Pérez Jiménez did not manage to live out his years in untroubled exile. At first, however, it appeared that he would go scot-free. Early in 1958, after he had staged a rigged plebiscite to prolong his one-man rule, he fled to an airport, dodging bullets from angered countrymen, and flew to the Dominican Republic. Two months later he went to live in a $400,000 Miami Beach mansion. In U.S. federal courts over the next few years he successfully fought extradition proceedings brought by the Venezuelan Government of Rómulo Betancourt. But late in 1962 his final court appeal was denied and he was jailed. The following year he was returned to Venezuela and indicted for having misused $13.5 million in Government funds.

The program of the coalition stressed the same basic issues advocated by *Acción Democrática* during its previous short period of power. The aim was essentially to create an economy in which all Venezuelans would enjoy decent living standards. In his Inauguration address in 1959, President Betancourt outlined some of the country's tangible problems. "The farm population for the most part lacks both credit and land," he said, "and its typical shelter is a primitive thatched hut with adobe walls and dirt floors, with no sanitary facilities whatever. Seven hundred thousand such dwellings constitute the sum total of housing for several million Venezuelans living in subhuman conditions."

Betancourt further listed more than two million illiterate adults—a third of the country's total population—about half a million school-age children without classrooms, barely 6,000 students in technical schools, an acute shortage of teachers and professors, and old, inadequate school buildings. "Infant mortality in the age group of one to four is ten times greater in Venezuela than in countries of advanced development. Almost every town lacks proper water supply and sewage facilities, and if their installations were to continue at the present rate, it would take a hundred years until these services could be offered to the entire population."

The reckless spending of the Pérez Jiménez years and the concurrent flight of capital from the country had depleted the treasury and bequeathed a financial crisis to the new regime. Its first concern was to restore international confidence. It cut back sharply on the grandiose building projects and drafted new policies for industrial development. Public funds were to be concentrated on basic industries such as electricity and steel. Secondary industry would be left to private enterprise insofar as possible, and foreign capital would be encouraged so long as it did not create monopolies contrary to the national interest.

Money shortages fortunately were not allowed to delay action on land distribution. A massive program was begun with the aid of funds supplied by the Alliance for Progress. In five years, 63,000 new family units were created on 4.2 million acres. The effect of these efforts at land reform was a significant reduction of social tension in the countryside. Although the recipients represented less than a sixth of the eligible families, the evidence of serious intent on the part of the Government created a willingness to wait more patiently. In this sense, the short-term results were excellent. What was less clear was the long-term success.

The new landowners had been organized in 700 cooperative settlements designed to supply machinery and other services. At the end of the five years, however, only nine of the settlements were producing satisfactorily. A shortage of technical assistance and of credit for seed and equipment had forced some of the peasants to abandon their farms. Others complained that the farms were too small to permit production beyond the family's immediate needs. These defects forced a slowing down of the rate of distribution so that the Government could devote more time and money to providing housing, credit, equipment, extension services, fertilizers and marketing facilities to the groups already settled.

Despite such partial setbacks, President Betancourt after five years in office was able to report gratifying progress. The annual increase in the gross national product during his term had been at a rate of 4.5 per cent. Further, expansion in the oil sector had been only 1.5 per cent, while agriculture had increased by 6.5 per cent and industry by 8 per cent. This reduction in the relative importance of oil represents a structural improvement in the Venezuelan economy. Betancourt was also able to report a better

A CASTRO THREAT IN VENEZUELA

When it was most threatened by Left-Wing terrorists, Venezuela's democratic Government rallied world opinion to its side by showing that the terrorists were abetted by the Cuba of Fidel Castro. On December 3, 1963, the Council of the Organization of American States met in emergency session in Washington to hear Venezuelan charges that Cuba had supplied arms to rebels trying to overthrow President Rómulo Betancourt's regime and halt the election of his successor. The election had been held two days before the OAS meeting, in an atmosphere tense from months of bombings, shootings, kidnapings and hijackings by pro-Communists. Venezuela charged that it had found a three-ton cache of arms sent from Cuba. After investigations 15 of the 20 OAS members voted to isolate Cuba by severing relations and applying economic sanctions.

distribution of the national wealth. Labor's share of the total national income rose from 45.5 per cent in 1958 to 59.7 per cent in 1962.

The extreme Right had brought about the downfall of the first *Acción Democrática* regime. The biggest threat to the second came from the opposite side. Over the years, Betancourt had withdrawn farther and farther from his early flirtation with Marxism, and as President he advocated close cooperation with the United States and urged full support of the Alliance for Progress. The Communists had joined the other parties in the pact to overthrow Pérez Jiménez. It was a short-lived alliance. Soon the Communists tried to transform the sentiment against the dictator into class warfare. In 1962 they joined with some disgruntled elements in the armed forces in an abortive revolt. Then they organized a terrorist organization in the cities, in the universities and in the countryside.

When it became clear that Fidel Castro's regime in Cuba was backing the terrorism in Venezuela, President Betancourt broke diplomatic relations with Cuba and brought charges against Castro before the Organization of American States. The response of the terrorists was a stepped-up campaign designed to prevent the holding of the Presidential elections scheduled for December 1963. The terrorists intended to discredit democracy by forcing a military coup.

Betancourt stood firm and kept the armed forces in line. With their help he rounded up hundreds of extremists, broke the terror campaign and held elections on schedule. The *Acción Democrática* candidate Raúl Leoni was elected President. The party's strength in Congress was reduced but it continued to be the biggest party and it formed a Government in a coalition with some smaller groups. Hope remained high that the age of democracy in Venezuela had truly dawned.

Venezuelan dictator Marcos Pérez Jiménez (center) dedicates a military school in January of 1958, shortly before he was deposed.

A Vigorous Attempt at Progress and Democracy

Venezuela is attempting simultaneously to forge a functioning democracy and a forward-looking culture—with relatively little tradition in either. For years the nation suffered alternately from anarchy and dictatorship, culminating in the brutal seven-year rule of Pérez Jiménez *(above)*. But after 1958, guided by Pérez Jiménez' longtime enemy Rómulo Betancourt, the country had constitutionally elected Governments. The new democracy created by Betancourt and his followers has been continually challenged from both Right and Left. But despite the often violent opposition, the new Governments have moved vigorously to use the nation's oil wealth to benefit their people. At the same time the vigor of the country's politics is paralleled by its current cultural life and especially by its advanced architecture.

THE MILITARY JUNTA that ousted a democratic Government in 1948 assembles on the first anniversary of its coup at Miraflores Palace, Caracas *(right)*. Second from left is Pérez Jiménez. He emerged to become a dictator whose rule was marked by brutal suppression of all political opposition and heavy profiteering by Government officials and foreign companies.

THE JUBILANT POPULACE takes to the streets *(above)* to celebrate Pérez Jiménez' departure from Venezuela early in 1958 following days of strikes and riots. He was eventually extradited from Miami to stand trial for his misdeeds in office.

A NEW JUNTA, made up of representatives from business and the military *(left),* takes over the shambles of government left by Pérez Jiménez in 1958. Within a year the junta held the elections in which Rómulo Betancourt became President.

INAUGURATING AN ERA, Rómulo Betancourt addresses the nation in 1959 as he assumes the Presidency after a year of rule by the junta that followed the durable Pérez Jiménez dictatorship. Betancourt took up reforms that had been begun before the time of Pérez Jiménez, and went on to become Venezuela's first honestly elected President to complete a term.

A QUEUE OF VOTERS, carefully guarded *(above)*, defies Leftist terrorists who had warned citizens to boycott the 1963 elections. Some 90 per cent of the electorate cast ballots.

BETANCOURT'S SUCCESSOR, Raúl Leoni, works at his desk shortly before winning the 1963 Presidential election *(below)*. He was Betancourt's personal choice for the office.

A PYRE OF SMOKE rises above a bus that was set afire by Betancourt opponents as a new wave of violence overtook Caracas during a telephone workers' strike in November 1960.

A BAND OF GUERRILLAS, modeling themselves on Fidel Castro's rebels, gathers in a clearing in 1963 *(above)*. They were part of a self-styled army of liberation against Betancourt.

A FEMINIST, Margot Boulton de Bottome brings Venezuela's women into the mainstream of political life

TALKING POLITICS, Mrs. Margot Boulton de Bottome *(right, second from left)* meets with women from the Frente Nacional Democrática, a conservative party.

ADDRESSING A GROUP that she founded, Intercambio, Venezuela's first women's club, Mrs. Bottome leads a discussion. She was also on Venezuela's U.N. delegation.

ENJOYING HER HOME LIFE, Mrs. Bottome listens *(left)* as her daughter Bolivia plays old folk songs on a traditional Venezuelan instrument known as a *quatro.*

ESCAPING FROM WORK, Mrs. Bottome joins her husband, a U.S. businessman, and friends on the beach *(opposite)* at their country home on the island of Margarita.

A GREAT ARCHITECT, *Carlos Raúl Villanueva*
influences the advanced design of his country's cities

PRECIOUS ART OBJECTS surround Carlos Raúl Villanueva in the home he built in Caracas' La Florida district. The works are by noted artists like the Spanish painter Joan Miró.

GRACEFUL HAMMOCKS are enjoyed by Villanueva and his wife at their second home at Caraballeda near the Caribbean *(opposite)*. Cross ventilation makes air conditioning unnecessary.

ADMIRING DISCIPLES gather about the master as he discourses on playground design at the Central University in Caracas *(below)*. Villanueva designed the university's buildings.

AN AIRY STUDIO where Villanueva works at his La Florida house serves as planning center for new projects. Either as the actual architect or as an adviser, he has had a hand in most of the modern public, apartment and office buildings that dominate Caracas.

115

8

The Varied Guianas

PRESIDENT Charles de Gaulle of France offered a good scientific reason for his 1964 decision to build a missile-launching site in French Guiana. The extra thrust of the spinning earth near the equator reduces the rocket power needed for lift-off. But cynics suggested that the availability of volunteers for space launchings was the real reason behind de Gaulle's decision. "If you're stuck in Cayenne," they said, "you'd go anywhere."

The availability of unused land undoubtedly also influenced the selection. Excluded from the Sahara proving grounds it had used before, France needed a new location for nuclear and other scientific experiments. French Guiana is bigger than the state of Maine, and the nine tenths of it that is covered by tropical forest is virtually unpeopled. Most of its 35,000 inhabitants live on the coast, more than half of them in the city of Cayenne.

Like Paramaribo and Georgetown, the capitals respectively of neighboring Surinam and of British Guiana, Cayenne lies on a low coastal plain, close to a shark-infested sea which is ocher-tinted by countless tons of Amazon silt which ocean currents wash along the Guiana shore. The three cities have a good deal in common. Located near the equator, they experience high humidity during two rainy seasons. Average precipitation at Georgetown is 92 inches—more than twice as much as New York City

—and the rain increases as one goes southeast along the coast to 140 inches a year at Cayenne. Temperatures are monotonously uniform in the eighties. In contrast with the often cloudy skies are the brilliant flowers—orchids, bougainvillaea, poinsettia and Indian lotus lilies. The sounds are the ever-present voice of the kiskadee bird and the incessant family squabbles of green parrots.

OF these three cities, Paramaribo is most clearly stamped with the qualities of the European power that built it. Its order and cleanliness are those of Holland. Many races have here achieved a working harmony while keeping their native languages, costumes and customs. Only 10 minutes away from modern concrete and glass buildings, Asiatic Indians work knee-deep in the muddy waters of their rice paddies and sarong-wrapped Javanese women sway gracefully toward their palm-shaded huts.

In Georgetown, a British atmosphere is maintained by the gingerbread architecture of the long-dead Victorian and Edwardian eras. Here one is more conscious than in Paramaribo of the distance between rich and poor. In town the English tend to act like the pukka sahibs of old, giving fancy-dress balls and playing cricket, but the roads to the city are lined with unpainted shacks on stilts which are as crowded as rabbit warrens. There are numerous canals of dirty water in which men fish, women launder and boys splash happily.

Cayenne is distinguished from the other two capitals by being on a slightly higher segment of the coastal plain. Its only other boast is an avenue of 90-foot-high palms which preside over rusty tin roofs on which the rain pounds endlessly through the long wet season. Ancient French-colonial homes and stores are warped, sagged and weatherbeaten behind the rusted grillwork of ornate balconies. Buzzards alight with a lazy double bounce and scavenge the sidewalks without conviction. The civil servants who constitute the town's main work-force close their offices for the day at 1 o'clock, postponing for the morrow a decision on the development programs which litter their desks. So it has always been in French Guiana, a country long habituated to being poised for take-off to greatness. Its history is one of hopeful starts and sad abortions.

The French landed at Cayenne in 1604 and settled permanently some 20 years later. The tropical coast seemed more attractive to some of their explorers than the frozen wastes of Canada to which their empire-building competitors were then confining them in North America. Earlier, they had gained a foothold at Rio de Janeiro in Brazil only to be expelled by the Portuguese. At Cayenne they did not do much better. The Dutch boxed them in by occupying northeastern Brazil, which lay to the south, and the Essequibo estuary to the northwest. They lost possession of French Guiana entirely several times, to the Dutch, the British and others.

Large-scale immigration was first attempted in the middle of the 18th Century. The spot selected for the first group of newcomers was the same one recently picked by de Gaulle for his rocket launching pad, an area between Kourou and Sinnamary on the coast. The recruiting agents beat the drums not only in France but also in Germany, Switzerland, Ireland and Canada. Thousands signed up—farmers, tradesmen, tricksters, ladies of fortune, even actors. Some, confused about French Guiana's location, brought their ice skates.

They also brought their diseases to add to those awaiting them. Dysentery, syphilis, yellow fever and malaria took a quick toll. The immigrant camps became hospitals, then cemeteries. The living could not bury the dead. Within a few months the survivors fled, 6,000 of them out of an estimated 14,000.

IN the following years a number of Negro slaves were imported and sugar plantations began to flourish. A setback occurred in 1794 when Revolutionary France abolished slavery. The colonists, however, quickly introduced a system of forced labor little different from slavery, and after only eight years legal slavery was re-established.

France's Second Republic, established by another revolution, in 1848, again decreed the abolition of slavery and this time it stuck, bringing a crisis for the sugar planters of French Guiana. The planters imported workers from India and China, but these Asians quickly found rural living intolerable and moved to the towns and became small traders and shopkeepers. To solve the impasse, France began in 1852 to send out long-term convicts, promising them that if they worked hard and behaved tolerably they would ultimately be released and allowed to become colonists. They came for 87 years, 70,000 of them in all. Some were confined on the three islands that are collectively known to all moviegoers as Devil's Island. But most were scattered in work camps in the mainland jungle, where they were exposed to malaria and yellow fever. Their net contribution was negligible. Only a handful survived to settle as farmers or tradesmen and establish families.

A MAJOR gold strike on the Approuague River in 1855 brought a new flurry of immigrants, and gold has been the main inducement for those who have since entered French Guiana of their own accord. Most of them have been West Indian Negroes. Many came from Martinique in 1902 when a volcanic eruption destroyed a town there. Some also have come from the British island of St. Lucia and continue to be known as the "English." English they were not, but they fitted easily into the racial mixture of French Guiana, where a large proportion of the population is made up of *métis*, or mixed-bloods. These mixed-blood people have now virtually absorbed the descendants of the Indians from India who were imported in the 19th Century. The original, indigenous Indian population has long since been decimated. Two centuries ago there were perhaps 20,000 Indians in the area of French Guiana; today there are about 1,200.

After World War II, French Guiana was made a Department of France, electing a senator and a deputy to sit in Paris. In political theory it ceased to be a colony and began to enjoy the benefits of equality with other French Departments. In principle it should have shared at least some of France's subsequent expansion and renewal. In fact, it shared little but France's rising costs of living.

Indeed, French Guiana is one of the world's most depressed areas. The cacao, indigo, cotton and spice plantations of the last century have totally disappeared, and sugar-cane plantations barely survive. In 1830, French Guiana exported twice what it imported, but by the 1960s exports paid for only one seventeenth of imports. There were only a third as many cattle as there had been a century earlier. Gold production had dropped from five tons a year to

about a quarter of a ton. The only significant exports aside from gold were shrimp and pineapples, but the shrimp-fishing industry was controlled by two United States companies. French Guiana had become a land of bureaucrats. Of approximately 7,000 wage earners, the state employed 4,000 as civil servants, teachers, policemen and public workers.

One curious and paradoxical factor which has contributed to French Guiana's current depression is that its coastal plain is above sea level and can be farmed without the elaborate systems of dikes and canals which are necessary in British Guiana and Surinam, and without advanced machinery. The result has been that the farming techniques in French Guiana have remained primitive. A more important factor which has contributed to the backwardness of French Guiana is simple lethargy. The region's enterprise seems to have been sapped by a dependence first on slave labor and then on a work-force of convicts. A population of only 35,000 must be fed with imported food, while the farmers of Surinam feed ten times, and those of British Guiana twenty times, as many people.

THE first settlers in what are now Surinam and British Guiana did not attempt to utilize the coastal swamps at all. Interested in trading with the Indians and afraid of Caribbean pirates, they selected sites some distance up the rivers. They found the land along the banks suitable for tobacco, cotton, coffee and cocoa. They also found very soon that tropical clays quickly lose their fertility when the natural vegetation is removed. In addition, competition from Virginia and Louisiana was making the cultivation of tobacco and cotton unprofitable, and the river banks were not suitable for sugar, the product most in demand.

It was at this point that interest in the coastal flats developed. Built up over scores of centuries by Amazon silt, the coast's alluvial soils were inexhaustibly fertile, although sea water had prevented the growth of plants other than mangrove and coarse saline grasses. But the Dutch had long been accustomed to dealing with similar problems along their own coastline, and they gradually worked out appropriate techniques. Sea walls with floodgates were built to control the tides. Dikes on the land side similarly held back flood waters after rain. Two levels of canals crisscrossed the enclosed area, the upper carrying irrigation water, the lower draining excess water and carrying barges for moving the crops to port or processing plant.

The high costs of installing and maintaining this water-control system were compensated for by high yields, and the growing of sugar cane became a profitable enterprise. Horse-drawn barges move more rapidly than ox-drawn carts, and this permitted an expansion of the growing area served by each cane-processing factory. The bigger production unit in turn encouraged more sophisticated machinery, so that the Guianas remained competitive with the West Indian sugar islands.

The industry prospered, but many planters did not. Heavy capital outlays forced them to borrow, and the weaker operators were absorbed by their competitors during the recurring depressions. British Guiana, where the planters had adopted the Dutch methods, had 380 estates by 1800, but the number had dropped to 230 in 1829, 180 in 1849 and 64 in 1896. Despite this shrinkage, British Guiana's sugar production increased more than 20 times during the century. Production again rose some 300 per cent between 1900 and 1960, but the number of separately administered sugar-growing operations dwindled to 12, 10 of them controlled by one firm, Bookers. Originally a Liverpool trading company, Bookers entered British Guiana as a distributor of merchandise, but the company gradually got into the sugar business by taking over the estates of defaulting debtors. Today it dominates British Guiana's industry, shipping, insurance, and wholesale and retail trade.

Sugar has equally dominated the social structure of British Guiana. Negro slaves supplied the hand labor for planting, cutting and grinding until the abolition of slavery in the second quarter of the 19th Century. The Colonial administration wanted to keep this labor force on the estates under a system of obligatory labor known as "apprenticeship," but the freed slaves naturally wanted to set up as independent farmers. To replace the Negro laborers, the British (and to a lesser extent the Dutch) recruited men from all over the world. They came from the West Indian islands, Germany, China, India, West Africa, the island of Madeira, Britain itself and even the United States. The Asiatic Indians proved the most useful laborers on the estates. The others succumbed to disease or moved to easier work in the towns. The Portuguese from Madeira, for example, 32,000 in all, acclimated quickly, but then moved into retail trade. Today their descendants form an important element in mercantile society.

BECAUSE they were the best workers in the sugar-cane fields, and because their own homeland was so poor, more Indian laborers were persuaded to immigrate than any other kind. By the time officially sponsored immigration was stopped in 1917, 250,000 Asiatic Indians had come to British Guiana (another 35,000 were imported by Surinam). However, even the Indians, accustomed as they were to hard labor in high temperatures, fell victim to

THE FEARSOME BEASTS OF THE GUIANAS

The rivers and forests of the Guianas contain some of the most ferocious and grotesque animals to be found anywhere on earth. Hunters who have ventured into the Guiana interior say that the problem is not to find game but to avoid being eaten by it. Some of these fearsome animals—such as the sharp-toothed piranha fish, which in schools can reduce a cow to a skeleton in minutes—are relatively well known. A few of the Guianas' lesser-known freaks—most of them vicious—are briefly described below.

THE PINGO is a savage pig that weighs more than 60 pounds and often travels in packs up to 200 strong. These packs move through the jungle en masse eating everything in their path, attacking hunting dogs and treeing the hunters.

THE BUSHMASTER, the largest venomous snake in the Americas, often reaches 12 feet in length. Its venom is not as toxic as that of some other snakes, but it is able to inject massive amounts of the venom through its extra-long fangs.

THE CAPYBARA, or "water pig," is a rodent that often grows to weigh 120 pounds, thus making it the largest rodent in the world.

THE ANACONDA is a river boa type of snake that lives in the Guianas' rivers. Growing as long as 25 feet, it is one of the world's two biggest snakes. It can easily squeeze the breath from a man.

THE MATAMATA TURTLE, the most grotesque of all the turtle order, looks like a repulsive clump of debris. Thus camouflaged it lies on river bottoms waiting for unwary fish. When a fish ventures near, the matamata sucks it in with a powerful vacuum device in its long, snakelike throat.

THE BLACK CAIMAN, which flourishes in the Guiana rain forest, is the fiercest and noisiest of all crocodiles. It will growl, bark and snort, and, on emotion-charged occasions, roar thunderously.

disease. The accommodations in the old slave quarters on the estates, surrounded by the near-stagnant waters of the canals, encouraged malaria, hookworm and other diseases. These ailments long outweighed the high fertility of the Indian women. Not until the 1920s did births begin to exceed deaths.

Nevertheless, the Asiatic Indian labor quickly revived sugar production in British Guiana and Surinam. Output hovered around 50,000 tons a year from 1840 to 1860 in British Guiana, then expanded rapidly for 25 years to 120,000 tons. But this period saw the expansion of Europe's sugar-beet industry and in 20 years, between 1875 and 1895, the price paid for raw sugar fell 50 per cent. Britain refused to help its Guianese planters, and they were saved only by the intervention of the United States, which by 1900 was taking three quarters of all the sugar produced in the Guianas and the West Indies.

The Spanish-American War proved a new disaster for the Guiana sugar industry. It brought Puerto Rico into the United States tariff area and gave Cuba and the Philippines, both sugar producers, large preferential margins. The industry in Surinam entered a decline from which it never recovered. In British Guiana it was saved by Canada's decision to give Guiana sugar privileged entry to its markets. When Britain joined Canada in the 1930s in according preferences, a new expansion began, and it continued when, after World War II, Britain introduced a system of quotas and guaranteed prices.

THE setback for sugar in the early 20th Century brought rice into prominence in both Surinam and British Guiana. The Asiatic Indians were traditionally rice-eaters, and they cultivated it successfully as a peasant crop. The coastal plain proved as suited to rice as to sugar cane. Production has risen even faster than population, supplying local needs and leaving a small export surplus.

The 20th Century also brought another income source. Both Surinam and British Guiana proved to have immense deposits of bauxite, the raw material of aluminum. By the early 1950s Surinam had become the world's leading producer, followed by British Guiana. Rapid expansion in Jamaica and the Soviet Union, however, subsequently dropped them to third and fourth place. British Guiana refines part of its bauxite into alumina (aluminum oxide) before export. Surinam in the mid-1960s will complete a large plant to process bauxite into alumina and the alumina into finished aluminum.

Sugar, rice and bauxite are thus the pillars of the economics of both Surinam and British Guiana. But the atmosphere in the two semi-independent colonies has been very different in the last decade and a half. Surinam has been largely peaceful, its competent rulers instituting intelligent and practical plans for both industrial and agricultural development. British Guiana, on the other hand, has suffered turmoil, bloodshed and at times an almost complete paralysis of industry and trade.

THE trouble in British Guiana began in 1953 when the colony was granted partial independence. The first election was won by the People's Progressive Party, which was led by an East Indian dentist-turned-politician named Cheddi Jagan. It quickly developed that Jagan, his forceful American-born wife and a number of his party lieutenants had decided leanings to the Left. What is more, Jagan and his P.P.P. almost immediately tried to destroy the nation's new Constitution and grab unlimited power for themselves. This the British Government would not tolerate, and it dispatched four warships and 1,600 troops to unseat Jagan and suspend independence. A royal commission appointed to study the situation reported that there was "no escape from the logical conclusion that so long as the present leadership and policies . . . continue, there is no way in which any real measure of self-government can be restored in British Guiana." The British resolved to push development programs designed to lessen the poverty-bred discontent that had made the Guianans easy prey for Jagan's rabble-rousing appeals.

Worse trouble descended on British Guiana about a decade later when the British once again decided their colony was ready to handle the responsibilities of independence. An election was held in 1961, and again Jagan won. Within six months his policies had inflamed the country. The root of the trouble this time was racial. Tension had been building between the country's East Indians, who were supporters of the East Indian Jagan, and the Negroes, who had found a leader in a London-educated Negro lawyer (and one-time ally of Jagan) named Forbes Burnham. The Negroes, who hate Jagan as a racist and Marxist, felt that he and his East Indians, given a free hand by Britain, would reduce them to peonage. The result was a Negro riot in February 1962 that destroyed whole sections of Georgetown. Jagan himself had to call in British troops to quell the rioters and impose peace.

Soon, however, the violence spread to the countryside. The British announced that new elections would be held, this time under a system of proportional representation which would hopefully exclude Jagan from the premiership. At this, Jagan supporters, hoping through violence to forestall such an election, dynamited irrigation canals, set fire to sugarcane fields and even bombed the homes of anti-Jagan Negroes. A general strike paralyzed all commerce.

Terrorism continued, flaring into an ugly race war in 1964 when Jagan, still hoping to forestall elections, sent gangs of East Indian sugar-cane workers into the country to bomb and shoot up Negro homes. The Negroes naturally retaliated, and in all some 170 people were killed and thousands injured.

Elections were held, however, and Jagan did indeed lose. The new Premier, Forbes Burnham, who in his youth had been thought to be a Communist, immediately sought aid and investment from the United States. Seeking peace at home, he invited East Indians to join his cabinet. Despite sporadic terrorism by followers of Jagan, British Guiana began slowly to get back on its feet. But the basic issues remained unresolved. Only a common fear held together a Government whose members had deeply conflicting interests. A high birth rate guaranteed that the Asiatic Indians would attain an absolute majority of the votes within a few years. In such unsettled circumstances, foreign capital was understandably reluctant to underwrite the economic expansion without which neither social nor political normality could be expected.

THE situation next door in Surinam has, fortunately, been very different. When Holland gave Surinam almost complete autonomy in 1954 the ex-colony's numerous and potentially antagonistic racial groups cooperated instead of fighting. The decline of the sugar industry in the early part of the century now proved to have been a blessing in disguise. It had produced a diversification of economic activity, more peasant farming, and less feeling of being in the stranglehold of alien interests. In addition, Holland followed through on a promise to give Surinam two guilders for every one Surinam could raise and thus helped launch a 10-year development plan. Tax incentives were offered foreign investors, who responded by starting half a dozen projects.

Surinam's 10-year plan has been cleverly designed and managed by the country's development ministry. One of the ministry's most successful schemes is what it calls "Operation Grasshopper." Perceiving that a thorough exploration on foot of Surinam's rain forest would take perhaps 80 years, the ministry decided to make an aerial survey. This mapping operation completed, airstrips were hacked out of the forest at strategic points so that geological survey teams could be flown in with their equipment. So far efforts to explore the forests have uncovered deposits of bauxite which contain hundreds of millions of tons of valuable ore. Meanwhile a subsidiary of the Aluminum Company of America called Suralco undertook to build a vast dam and hydroelectric works which will run a big aluminum plant and be of incalculable benefit to the Surinam economy.

ALL is not perfect in Surinam. There is danger of racial conflict—and virtually all political activity is divided by race. As in British Guiana, the birth rate of the East Indians is higher than that of the Negroes, and the Negroes suffer from a nagging fear that they are, or inevitably will be, pushed around. The overall birth rate is in itself a threat. The population is increasing faster than the growing economy, and the country's usually optimistic leaders sometimes admit that unemployment and other problems loom menacingly. But the elected representatives of the Asiatic Indians and of the Negroes work together, and more recently they brought the representatives of the Javanese into the coalition. This cooperation among politicians holds out the hope that the separate racial societies can continue to coexist peacefully and may ultimately fuse into a single multiracial society. Herein lies the solution not only for the Guianas' racial problems but for those of the world's other areas of festering bitterness as well.

Princess Beatrix of Holland greets an Amerindian on her 1965 tour of Surinam, an integral part of the Kingdom of the Netherlands.

An Era of Transition in the Colonial Enclaves

The Guianas, lingering colonial outposts, are in effect islands lying between the sea and the impenetrable Amazon jungle. Thus cut off from their Latin neighbors, they are closely bound up with their mother countries. Like Surinam, which is incorporated politically as a part of Holland, French Guiana is technically a department of France. Yet while Surinam is undergoing cultural and economic development on its own, the economically stagnant French colony lacks internal vitality. British Guiana, on the other hand, is well on the way to independence, a movement slowed down by local racial turmoil.

BALLET ROUTINES are practiced by Surinamese students in a dance class *(above)* at the Cultural Center in Paramaribo, the capital city. The center also has an art school and library.

HINDU WEDDING proceeds in traditional style in the interior, although the girl wears a Western bridal dress beneath her sari *(below)*. About 94,000 Asian Indians live in Surinam.

JAVANESE DANCING is performed in the countryside *(above)* on a Sunday afternoon. Surinam has 43,000 Javanese. They came as indentured servants in the years before World War II.

MODEST PROSPERITY makes
Surinam a stable colony and permits
a wide range of cultural activities

HIGH-GRADE BAUXITE lies in storage *(above)* at Moengo in eastern Surinam awaiting shipment. The mineral, the basis for Surinam's well-being, accounts for 80 per cent of its exports.

PROCESSING PLANT where bauxite is crushed lies on the Cottica River at Moengo *(left)*. It is one of two large plants owned by a subsidiary of the Aluminum Company of America.

AN AURA OF DECAY lies over towns of French Guiana, a colony that has seen relatively little progress

A LOCAL MATRON strolls past one of the weed-infested street gardens of St. Laurent du Maroni (*above*), a town that was a well-maintained penal colony until 1946. Today bushes grow in rain gutters and paint on houses is chipped and faded.

A SHADED BANDSTAND provides a convenient place for loafing in midafternoon in the center of Cayenne, capital of French Guiana *(above)*. Unlike British Guiana and Surinam, French Guiana is both politically and economically backward.

FRENCH SOLDIERS stroll past old St. Laurent prison buildings that have been turned into housing for the local populace *(left)*. Since 1946, when the colony became a department of France, most of the prisoners have been relocated elsewhere.

A FARM WIFE shoos chickens from her path outside her St. Laurent home *(right)*. Although there is much rich soil available in French Guiana, most food must be imported. There is also good local fishing, but fish, too, is an import item.

COLONIAL CRICKETERS representing several Guianan clubs practice for a forthcoming match with an Australian team. This session was held at the Georgetown Cricket Club, one of the many manifestations of the British presence. British interests also dominate the colony's economy, with the British-owned Booker Group controlling 10 of the 12 large sugar estates.

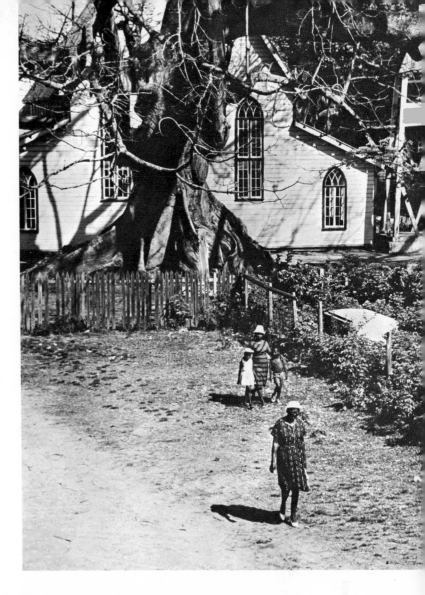

SMARTLY DRESSED SCHOOLGIRLS pass a sidewalk vendor in Georgetown, British Guiana's capital *(above)*. The department store in the background is a Booker Group holding.

GUIANAN CHRISTIANS leave a church nestled amid foliage *(right)*. Most of the colony's 190,000 Negroes are Christians; most of its 300,000 Asian Indians are Hindus or Moslems.

WORKERS' HOUSES raised above swampy ground occupy a field on a British-controlled coastal sugar estate *(below)*. Most of the sugar workers live in such homes or in nearby villages.

RACIAL CONFLICT has befouled the nationalist movement in British Guiana

SOCIALIST LEADER, Cheddi Jagan, whose People's Progressive Party is oriented toward his fellow Asian Indians, campaigns in the 1961 elections *(above)*. His party won, and he again became Premier of British Guiana. But violent opposition from the country's Negro minority brought economic troubles, causing Britain to postpone granting the colony independence.

CONTROVERSIAL CAMPAIGNER, Janet Jagan, Cheddi Jagan's American wife, talks with voters deep in the interior *(above)*. She held several high positions in her husband's Cabinet.

BRITISH TROOPS called in by Jagan march through riottorn Georgetown in February 1962 *(right)*. Jagan's opponents had claimed that he favored Asian Indians over the colony's Negroes, and also that his policies would lead to Communism. Demonstrations against him went on for two weeks; then looting and violence began. Two years later Jagan was out of office.

NEGRO SPOKESMAN, Forbes Burnham *(above)* brandishes a broom during the 1961 elections and shouts, "We will sweep them out," meaning the Jagan Government. The crowd waved back, chanting, "Keep them out!" In 1964 Burnham's People's National Congress, a party formed on racial lines, won enough votes to form a Government with the aid of a third party.

9

New Forces
in Education
and the Arts

ALEJANDRO OBREGON, one of Colombia's most influential painters, is professionally fond of fish. For a 1959 exhibition in Bogotá he chose 26 works inspired by the mojarra, an edible fish of the Caribbean. One woman journalist who reviewed the show expressed her approval in language that might seem ill-fitted to so prosaic a subject: "Obregón's variations . . . are pure poetic language."

Readers of the critique may have agreed or disagreed with the judgment, but they found nothing incongruous about the expression of it. Poetry is for Colombians the apex of all art and culture. To be worthy of his calling, even a painter of fish must have the soul of a poet. A favorite Colombian

saying runs, "for every hundred inhabitants, we have two hundred poets."

Education in both Colombia and Venezuela has traditionally been geared to this concept of poetry (and to a lesser degree, the other arts) as a culmination. The Spaniards brought from Europe the humanist ideal of the well-rounded gentleman who was equipped to do gracefully whatever he chose to attempt. The gentleman could manage his business affairs with aplomb, lead an army should the need arise, dabble in the arts when he had nothing more pressing to occupy his time, and, with casual grace, write poetry as the mark of his class. This ideal took deep root. It suited the image which the upper-class

Spaniard had of himself. It was, for that matter, a fairly practical notion while both the society and the economy remained simple, needing neither many educated leaders nor a variety of specialists.

The trouble is that such an ideal does not suffice as a society becomes more complex. The Italian humanists who elaborated this plan for the perfect education envisioned it as the training for a Renaissance prince, or at most for a small circle of 16th Century aristocrats. What nations need in the 20th Century, however, is many educated specialists—engineers, physicists, electricians, even government clerks—and a literate and informed electorate. A richly learned cultural aristocracy is a fine thing for any nation to have, but it is no longer enough. In Colombia and Venezuela, however, the old ideal of education only for a select elite has until recently prevailed, and it has served to inhibit the spread of education to the mass of the people.

World trends in the 19th Century made politicians in both countries pay lip service to the principle of universal schooling. Free obligatory primary education for all was decreed in 1870 by a Venezuelan dictator, Antonio Guzmán Blanco. He even made an effort to move toward this goal. His successors, however, lacked his enthusiasm. As recently as 1950, only 3.8 per cent of the Venezuelan people had had primary schooling.

BOTH Colombia and Venezuela have since embarked on ambitious plans to educate their people. They have undertaken extensive school-building and teacher-training programs. Venezuela's progress has been more remarkable than Colombia's, especially under the democratic regime installed in 1959. School and college enrollments rose from a little more than half a million in 1950 to a million in 1959, and to more than a million and a half in 1964. Adult-education campaigns made a further dent in the mass of illiterates.

The most hopeful sign of all, however, is the changing attitudes of the two countries' leaders. They no longer just talk about universal schooling; they believe in it. The old aristocratic ideal is dying, and these leaders have become convinced that progress requires an educational system geared to the needs of industry. Such countries as Colombia and

Venezuela nevertheless offer built-in obstacles to any educational advance.

The first obstacle is simply the lack of a proper climate for literacy. Many pupils come from homes where the parents do not read or write, where there are no tables at which to study, no shelves on which to store schoolbooks, no lights by which to read at night, no books, newspapers or even comic strips to stimulate interest and give literacy a purpose. Within a few years of leaving school, many of the students have forgotten whatever they were taught. Statistically literate, they are functionally illiterate.

A recent Venezuelan study stresses another of the obstacles. More than a quarter of the pupils drop out of school after the first year. One reason is the late starting age. A fourth of the students in the first grade were, according to the study, 10 to 14 years old. Students that old have a tendency to feel that the stiff and rather old-fashioned curriculum prescribed for Venezuelan schools has little relevance to their daily lives. Many, of course, have to drop out of school and seek jobs. Both countries lack classroom space; in Colombia 800,000 children between the ages of seven and 12 cannot be accommodated in schools.

Still another difficulty is the continuing inadequacy of teacher training. In Colombia 56 per cent of all primary teachers lack certification. The situation in Venezuela is considerably better, but it is clear that both nations must not only build a great many schools but also make the most strenuous efforts to staff them with competent instructors. The task of combating all these obstacles to simple literacy, let alone giving the mass of the people educations which will make them useful citizens in a modern society, seems all but impossible. But at least the need for action is recognized and some vigorous first steps have been taken.

CHANGE is also called for in the universities, where the grip of tradition, of the old humanist ideal, until recently remained strong. In the last few years a number of universities have expanded rapidly, and with expansion they have tried to alter their curricula, bringing them more in line with today's needs. But competent staffs and costly equipment are not assembled overnight. Nor do attitudes change, and an imbalance in the numbers of students following various fields of study remains acute. In Venezuela, as recently as 1962, 19 per cent of university students elected to study for the gentlemanly profession of law, but only 4.6 per cent chose to bend their eyes on the earth and study agronomy, and only 2.8 per cent chose other sciences.

University life in Colombia and Venezuela is also deformed by excessive student involvement in politics—as it is in many South American countries. Middle-class students especially, either from idealistic commitment or to further the interests of their class, have founded student movements and agitated for social change. Elections to student offices are bitterly contested, and this intramural politicking takes up a disproportionate share of the time and energy of many students. Campus riots are endemic, and student demonstrations against Government policies are a feature of public life.

The political enthusiasm of the university students has not, by and large, spread to the arts in Colombia and Venezuela. Sculptors and painters have remained far more aloof from the revolutionary struggle than their counterparts in Mexico and in many other countries. Why this is so is hard to say. Perhaps sophistication, in the best sense of the word, is part of the answer. Many artists feel that the concern of art is art and not politics, and that if an artist becomes committed to one social cause or another his art must inevitably cease to be an objective search for truth and become merely a high form of political propaganda. Perhaps, too, the very respect for the arts which is especially marked in this region of South America has contributed to this aloofness from the hurly-burly of politics and programs.

Not that Colombian and Venezuelan artists have been totally indifferent to social problems, or that

there have not been some painters who were influenced by the revolutionary artists of Mexico. In the 1930s Luis Alberto Acuña, Pedro Nel Gómez and others devoted their paintings to the grievances of workers and Indians. Acuña's Colombian peasant faces, in particular, evoke the work of the famous Mexican painters Orozco, Siqueiros and Rivera. The trend did not last, but the work of these painters did have beneficial effects on Colombian and Venezuelan art as a whole. It helped to dramatize the inadequacy of the region's traditional styles of painting, especially the 19th Century Bolívar-on-horseback school, and it sent painters off to Europe and North America for inspiration and instruction.

When these painters, who had absorbed the latest trends and techniques in the world's art capitals, returned to their homelands, the initial public reaction was chilling. The public made an unusually swift about-face, however, and soon the work of these men was being accepted and praised. The career of Alejandro Obregón is characteristic. Having studied in the School of the Museum of Fine Arts in Boston, Obregón returned to Bogotá in 1943 to find himself and his work totally ignored. His first show was noted in the press only because a vandal had slashed a picture of a nude. Obregón, a member of a wealthy family, could afford to ignore his ignorers. Acting and dressing like a Bohemian, he continued to paint and soon won attention. Allies appeared in the form of Bogotá's students, who campaigned against the academic traditionalists and succeeded in having them thrown out of their key teaching and administrative positions. In 1948 Obregón, at the age of 27, became director of the city's School of Fine Arts.

Colombian painters who have since joined Obregón as top exponents of the new styles include Fernando Botero, Guillermo Weidemann, Eduardo

THE INDIANS' ARTISTRY IN GOLD

The masterly goldwork produced by several of the Indian cultures which thrived in the Colombian Andes before the Spanish conquest constitutes one of Latin America's artistic treasures. The goldwork of several of these cultures is briefly described below.

THE CALIMA specialized in large, heavy body ornaments, often embellished with geometric motifs. Much of this work, and that of other cultures, can be seen in the Gold Museum in Bogotá.

THE QUIMBAYA made fluted flasks and other vessels of gold of extreme delicacy and purity of design.

THE CHIBCHA made "tunjos" or flat, stylized human figures with elongated bodies, large heads and decorations of gold wire.

THE TOLIMA made magnificent cast-gold pendants, usually in the shape of an anchor but with stylized human heads on their tops.

Ramírez Villamizar and Enrique Grau. Unlike Obregón, they avoid controversy, wearing rather the mantle of professional men. They leave parties early, pleading that they must work in the morning. And they make good livings. Botero expresses the change in public attitudes. "We are on the first page of the newspapers," he has said, "and as famous as local football players. Where else but modern Colombia could this happen?"

T HESE painters have evolved distinctive styles which do not fit comfortably into any one category. German-born, Weidemann did representational painting of the Negro culture of the Pacific coast when he settled in Colombia in 1939, but later changed to Abstract Expressionism. Ramírez Villamizar, along with the sculptor Edgar Negret, is fascinated by machinery. This has led Ramírez Villamizar, a one-time student of architecture, to a stark, geometric style. Negret says that Latin Americans have two attitudes toward art—a religious or magical approach to landscape, and a wonder at machines. He combines them in his sculptures, which he calls "magic machines."

Fernando Botero calls himself a Neofigurativist; his specialty is doing satirical and amusing variations on Leonardo da Vinci's *Mona Lisa*. Best known is the *Mona Lisa at 12,* an overfed, self-satisfied caricature of Da Vinci's masterpiece. Enrique Grau is also a representational painter, although he began as an Abstractionist. His paintings of women appear curiously lighthearted, as if he took neither women nor the craft of painting very seriously.

Painting in Venezuela followed a path parallel to Colombia's, but today it has become more daringly avant-garde. The break with the old tradition was made in the 1920s by Armando Reverón, who died in 1954. He progressed from a Spanish academic style through vague French Impressionism to a personalist position distinguished by an ever-lighter palette. Working on such fragile or eccentric materials as wrapping paper and burlap, and using homemade paints, he ended up with pictures which were almost bone-white except for shadowy details.

Reverón was followed by a number of revolutionary young painters, some of whom formed a group called "The Dissidents." All strongly influenced by contemporary Parisian currents, The Dissidents proclaimed their beliefs in a manifesto published in Paris in 1950. "Our watchword is *No,*" they declared. "*No* to the false salons of Official Art. . . . *No* to the false art critics. . . . *No* to the newspapers which back such absurdities and to the public which goes unprotesting each day to the slaughterhouse."

The Dissidents and other young artists began to show their work during the 1950s and their capture of the art world of Venezuela was soon complete. The most notable craftsman among The Dissidents was Alejandro Otero. His experiments in Geometric Abstraction strongly influenced many of his contemporaries. He has won praise not only in Venezuela but in the world's art capitals as well. Other experimental artists include Jesús Soto, Héctor Poleo, Humberto Jaimes, Elsa Gramcko and Carlos Contramaestre. They remain very much under the influence of Paris and New York. Some of them seek to shock by gluing all sorts of junk on their canvases. Soto was one of the first artists to experiment with Op Art. His pictures, Soto says, constitute "a visual experience." Contramaestre pieces his works together with animal bones, rags—especially old brassières—bits of newspaper and other objects to produce what have been appropriately labeled "nauseating" pictures. Héctor Poleo explores the terrible, the absurd and the grotesque. Characteristic of Poleo's work is a self-portrait in which he imagines himself in old age—a shriveled, sightless old man waiting dumbly for death to snatch him.

A RCHITECTURE is another area in which Venezuelans have excelled. Oil revenues in the 1940s and 1950s permitted public works on a grandiose scale. The first high-rise buildings were uninspired. With the midcentury, however, Venezuela began to make architectural news, largely because of the distinctive new designs using reinforced concrete developed by Carlos Raúl Villanueva. His public housing projects and civic structures have transformed adobe-and-red-tiled Caracas into one of the most modern of South America's cities. In his most important work, the University City of Caracas, Villanueva designed everything from the concert hall to the library to the sports stadiums. One of the most interesting aspects of Villanueva's architecture is his bold and successful integration of art and architecture. In his University City buildings he has included murals, stained-glass windows, sculpture and mosaics.

Tradition hangs more heavily on Colombian architecture. Although the Swiss-French architect Le Corbusier was commissioned to make a master plan for Bogotá's development in 1949, his suggestions for opening up the quaint colonial city were followed in a disorganized way. Most Colombian cities are still characterized by the architecture of the colonial era. Their skyscrapers are uninspired transplants from Chicago or Dallas. The area of most successful experimentation is the suburban villa, simpler and more functional than the old patio-dominated town house, but clinging to tradition in its grilled ironwork, colored tiles and graceful arches.

LITERATURE in Colombia and Venezuela has had no renaissance in modern times comparable to that of the plastic arts. There has been, however, a considerable amount of writing, some of it of high quality, and a love of and respect for literature is reflected in flourishing bookstores which offer an impressive array of the world's treasures.

Poetry continues to inspire the most interest in Colombia, partly, no doubt, because the country produced in this century one of Latin America's truly fine poets, Guillermo Valencia. A diplomat as well as a poet, Valencia wrote verse which is both lofty in tone and highly polished in technique. His concern for perfection of form grew out of a deep knowledge of the Greek and Latin classics and earned Valencia his countrymen's acclaim as *El Maestro*. Valencia's influence on other Colombian poets, even since his death in 1943, has been pervasive and largely explains why, instead of writing about the life of their beautiful and troubled country, they have concentrated on verbal perfection.

Yet poetry remains an abiding interest of all literate Colombians. Newspapers bulge with poems and with columns about poetry, all very erudite and grandiloquent and full of classical references. Radio stations have flourishing poetry programs. A trade union finds nothing incongruous in promoting a poetry contest among its members. Yet when all assessments are rendered, only Valencia among Colombia's 20th Century poets has yet climbed Parnassus.

The poets cannot, however, be accused of living solely in a world of metaphor and meter. The typical poet is also a fiction writer, an essayist, a journalist and a critic of both literature and art. A study of the novel in Colombia published in 1957 listed 747 titles, 262 published in the previous 27 years. Only two Colombian novels, however, have won lasting acclaim, *María* (1867) by Jorge Isaacs, and *La vorágine* (1924; translated into English as *The Vortex*) by José Eustasio Rivera. Isaacs was the son of a prosperous English Jew who settled in Colombia. His largely autobiographical novel is a masterpiece of the Romantic school. The hero Efraín returns from boarding school to fall in love with his beautiful cousin. The family is opposed to the marriage on religious grounds and the impasse is resolved only by the cousin's death. *La vorágine* is a very different book, as tough and realistic as *María* is romantic. Rivera, a lawyer as well as a poet and novelist, was appointed secretary of a commission in 1922 to settle a boundary dispute between Colombia and Venezuela. His experiences in the Amazon jungle country inspired *La vorágine*, which describes the exploitation of highland people recruited to work on rubber plantations in the steaming rain forest.

A FEW other Colombian novelists deserve notice. Tomás Carrasquilla provides a realistic account of the life of a family in the industrial city of Medellín in *Frutos de mi tierra* (1896; the title means "Fruits from My Land"). Carrasquilla, who died in 1940, was a master of realistic dialogue. César Uribe Piedrahita, a doctor, archeologist and art collector as well as a writer, has written a realistic story of the oil fields called *Mancha de aceite* ("Oil Stain," 1935). Another effective Colombian novel is *Una derrota sin batalla* ("Beaten without a Fight") which was written in 1933 by Enrique Pardo Farelo, who signed his work as Luis Tablanca. A political satire, it describes two idealists who resign from public office after five days because of their disgust with unscrupulous and deceitful politicians. The point of Tablanca's satire is that the average Colombian expects politicians to be deceitful and unscrupulous, and therefore does not fight against corruption in government.

In Venezuela, where the novel predominates over poetry, one novelist overshadows his fellow writers both in his homeland and in Colombia. This is the remarkable Rómulo Gallegos, who was elected President of Venezuela in 1947. His best-known novel, *Doña Bárbara* (1929), has been translated into many languages including English and has almost reached the status of compulsory reading for all Spanish-speaking students. The novel presents the semibarbarous, dictator-dominated society of rural Venezuela as a symbol of what must be purged from national life to make Venezuela a fully civilized country. Now in his eighties, Gallegos is a much-venerated citizen. A stamp was issued in his honor, a Government-sponsored literary prize was named for him, and he was the first recipient of a recently created honor, the Order of Caracas.

Three other significant Venezuelan novelists are Arturo Uslar Pietri, Miguel Otero Silva and Antonio Arraiz. Intensely active as diplomat, politician and university professor, Uslar Pietri pours out an endless flow of essays, short stories and socioeconomic studies. His best novel is *Las lanzas coloradas* (1931), which has recently been translated into English as *Scarlet Lances*. Written in a remarkable poetic prose, it is a lyrical evocation of the Wars of Independence. Otero Silva, a millionaire newspaper publisher and Senator, writes at a more leisurely pace than Uslar Pietri. Among his best works are *Casas muertas* ("Dead Mansions," 1955), which describes the effects of dictatorship on Venezuelan society, and a striking study of the social problems of the Venezuelan oil fields called *Oficina número 1* ("Office Number 1," 1961). His 1939 novel *Fiebre* ("Fever") anatomizes some of the horrors of Juan Vicente Gómez's long dictatorial regime and has helped many Venezuelans to understand the dangers of dictatorship. This is also true of a powerful realistic novel called *Puros hombres* ("Real Men") by Antonio Arraiz, also published in 1939. Arraiz was a political prisoner in one of Gómez's jails for seven years, an experience he describes with considerable force as somewhat less than pleasant.

UNLIKE Colombia and Venezuela, the Guianas never had a resident cultured class with the time and inclination to develop the arts. The pursuits of the wealthy were strictly practical. Government officials and businessmen alike were birds of passage. Even those who settled for a number of years thought of their roots as being in Europe. There they sent their children to school, and there they eventually retired with what wealth they had amassed.

Primitive living conditions and European influences tended to destroy whatever folk culture was brought to the Guianas by the workers imported from other parts of the world. This is particularly evident in British Guiana. Almost all Negro folk art has vanished except music and dance, and even these tend to follow the leadership of the West Indian islands. The Asiatic Indians have largely forgotten their homeland's languages, and the picturesque processions and rituals of India have decayed pathetically.

French Guiana's main contribution to art was a series of frescoes by a counterfeiter named Francis La Grange who was imprisoned on one of the group of islands popularly known as Devil's Island. Since the penitentiary was closed shortly after World War II, the frescoes, which depict incidents from the life of Christ, have rotted in the abandoned chapel. After his release, La Grange settled in Cayenne, where he did a series of tableaux recording his prison life. The originals were sold to an American visitor, but duplicates made by La Grange from his originals are on view in a Cayenne restaurant.

SURINAM'S various racial groups retain more of their heritage. While British and French colonizers have imposed their languages as a unifying element, the Dutch thrive in a multilingual situation. Several Asiatic Indian languages and Javanese flourish in Surinam alongside Dutch and English, and each racial group maintains its own ways.

The growing middle class of Negroes and Asiatic Indians in British Guiana and Surinam is now seeking art forms to express the emotions of these emerging nations. British Guiana has produced some worthwhile novelists, and Georgetown boasts a center where painters, sculptors, dancers and actors indulge in their lively arts. Paramaribo's similar center spreads its ambition even wider to embrace a symphony orchestra and a ballet school. They not only dream of but prepare for the coming of a statue, a painting, a song or a dance that will have in it the special heartbeat of the new nation.

On the road to literacy, Pedro Emilio Oviedo writes diligently in a notebook at a new school in Zipaquira, Colombia, near Bogotá.

The Opening Up of Broader Cultural Horizons

In the past, learning and art in Colombia and Venezuela amounted to little more than a European-style education for the rich, a connoisseurship of the arts on the part of the privileged. The poor were illiterate. But just as northern South America has recently seen a ferment of new social, political and economic theories, so has it awakened to the possibilities of broadening its culture and extending it to a large segment of the population. Universal education is now an officially proclaimed goal in both Colombia, where by law 10 per cent of the budget goes to education, and Venezuela, whose democratic governments have sharply reduced illiteracy. Moreover, although such efforts are still in an early stage, the expansion of education in the two nations has coincided with a sparkling explosion in the creative arts.

NEW FACILITIES help expand an educational system once designed only for the elite

A PRIMARY SCHOOL near Bogotá, put together with prefabricated walls *(left)*, helps alleviate Colombia's critical classroom shortage. The building was financed with U.S. Alliance for Progress funds.

THE NEW CAMPUS that serves Caracas' old Central University was designed by Carlos Villanueva *(pages 114-115)* and presents one of the hemisphere's great modern architectural panoramas *(below)*.

MEDICAL STUDENTS lean forward to watch a physiology demonstration *(left)* at the Universidad del Valle in Cali, Colombia. With 23 universities, Colombia gives greater attention to higher education than to primary and secondary schooling.

AN ART CLASS meets in an appropriate setting in one of the attractive new classrooms at the Central University *(below)*. Tuition charges for higher education are modest, and sometimes such fees are nonexistent at Venezuela's seven universities.

LIVELY ARTS provide color and excitement in a region breaking loose from tradition

A BOLD PAINTER, Alejandro Obregón uses strong lines to heighten the emotion of his dreamlike still lifes. One of Colombia's best-known artists, he has exhibited extensively abroad.

AN IMAGINATIVE SCULPTOR, the young Colombian Alvaro Herrán transforms materials like brass *(above)* into graceful works of art. A former dentist, he is also a successful painter.

AMUSING SATIRIST, Fernando Botero of Colombia stands in front of one of his fat, smiling women *(above)*. He does similar paintings of priests. After studying in Europe, he exhibited in Colombia, the U.S. and Mexico.

CELEBRATED INNOVATOR, Marisol Escobar, a Venezuelan who uses only her first name, leans on a work *(opposite)* that combines painting with sculptured heads and instrument gauges. Marisol is well known in New York.

BRAVE NOVELIST, Rómulo Gallegos *(right)* sits before his typewriter in 1947, after he became President of Venezuela. He was soon overthrown by a Right-Wing junta. His writing, like his politics, emphasizes social justice.

10

A Slow Struggle toward the Sunlight

THE myth of El Dorado—the fabulous city of gold—is entitled to the place it occupies in world folklore because it illustrates a common experience of individuals and peoples. They look for imagined riches beyond the horizon while ignoring the real wealth at their feet.

With the possible exception of French Guiana, the lands of El Dorado seem today to have learned this lesson. They have stopped dreaming that somehow things will take care of themselves. They have become conscious that they must exploit with vigor and intelligence their considerable natural resources.

Colombia and Venezuela, independent republics for a century and a half, have developed the basic political forms and experience, and the sense of national identity, needed for such a task. The democratic political forms, however, have not yet been honored very much in practice. The privileged classes in Colombia have perfected a species of sleight of hand which makes it appear that democracy is at work while, in fact, they retain a monopoly of decision-making positions. In Venezuela the middle class has won a bigger voice in government, but this is partially offset by the need to weigh the views and protect the interests of the Army establishment when formulating public policy.

The Guianas are at a lower level of political evolution. Britain has agreed to grant British Guiana its independence once the internal situation gives promise that a broad-based democratic regime will follow. Bitter racial strife and the expressed pro-Marxism of Cheddi Jagan, the leader of the biggest political party, have lessened the likelihood that this condition can be met. British Guiana has its own elected Government, but Britain keeps a close watch on its doings and retains effective control. Some solution for this impasse must be found, for political uncertainty is an insuperable obstacle to capital investment and without investment progress is impossible.

The outlook for political stability is much better in Surinam, the former Dutch Guiana. Even though the racial groups remain separated from one another, as they do in British Guiana, their leaders have succeeded in finding common ground. In consequence, Surinam has moved out of the colonial era and enjoys virtual independence, although it accepts aid and advice from the Kingdom of the Netherlands.

FRENCH GUIANA has been thrust into a political limbo by being incorporated into France as a department. About all that can be said in favor of this arrangement is that no better one appears currently viable. Even in this era when dozens of tiny corners of the earth have become independent nations, nobody imagines that French Guiana's 35,000 people could go it alone on a mudbank where they survive only because their worse-than-depressed economy is underwitten by France.

For the moment, France seems willing for the sake of prestige to make the investment involved in keeping French Guiana afloat. But the flow of world politics could always alter the situation and leave the lethargic and poverty-stricken area isolated. It might then be absorbed by Brazil or possibly Surinam. Some people have suggested, for that matter, that it might be logical not just for Surinam to absorb French Guiana but for all three Guianas to fuse into a single nation. Their peoples are of similar racial backgrounds and have had comparable histories. They produce the same crops for the most part and export the same minerals. Together, they could bargain more effectively and plan a more rational exploitation of their resources, both human and material.

Up to now, nevertheless, no significant sentiment for unity has been visible. Each of the Guianas remains economically and culturally linked to a different European power. To spark change would require a major jolt, as for example, a decision by Venezuela to press its claim to nearly half the territory of British Guiana. Arbitration established the present boundary in 1899, granting Great Britain almost 90 per cent of the area then in dispute. Venezuela claims to have unearthed evidence that the arbitrators were biased and that the issue should be reopened. Were Venezuela to insist on annexation, it might send all three Guianas scurrying together in self-protection.

WHAT is certain is that Venezuela for the first time is making serious efforts to move into the border areas near British Guiana. It is convinced that in this region around the mouths of the Orinoco a significant part of its El Dorado of natural resources has been found. The obstacles that long prevented exploration and exploitation—disease, heat, humidity and floods—are finally controllable, thanks to 20th Century medicine and technology.

What first awakened Venezuela to the region's potential wealth was the discovery in the 1940s of rich iron deposits in and near the now-famous iron mountain, Cerro Bolívar. The total amount of ore probably exceeds a billion tons, and much of it is 58 per cent pure. United States interests dredged the nearby Orinoco River and built port facilities and railroads to get the ore out. The Venezuelan Government built a steel mill that is operated with hydroelectric power provided by the Caroní River, a tributary of the Orinoco. The city of Santo Tomé de Guayana was created in 1961 by combining two boomtowns which in 12 years had grown from 4,000 to 50,000 inhabitants. Here an industrial complex is being developed and the projected population of Santo Tomé for 1975 is 400,000, increasing to more than 600,000 in the 1980s. Venezuela's development program envisages production not only of primary metals and heavy machinery but also of pulp and paper products and construction materials. There is abundant cheap hydroelectricity, oil and gas are available from nearby fields, and the Orinoco offers freighters direct access to the Atlantic.

Venezuela can embark on such ambitious projects because of its earlier discovery of oil. The history of oil in Venezuela is a classic example of the complex process of modernizing a backward country. At first the profits from the oil went mostly to foreign companies and to a handful of politicians. Soon, however, some of this wealth began to trickle into the national economy. There it acted in much the same way as the flood of gold from its colonies had acted on Spain's economy centuries before; that is, it stifled native enterprise and weakened rather than strengthened the whole economic structure.

But the long-term effects in Venezuela were beneficial. The temporary weakening of the economy depressed agriculture and this broke the political power of the old landowning class. A new aristocracy of bankers, industrialists, professional men and builders came into prominence. The money economy increased the numbers and raised the status of the middle class. These new elements forced a constantly higher proportion of the oil income into the treasury, to be used for national progress. This money has recently underwritten a vast expansion of higher education. It has permitted the purchase of significant acreage for land distribution to peasants. It has gone into roads, harbors, irrigation, power production and industrialization.

COLOMBIA is not nearly as well situated as Venezuela for carrying out a similar modernization of its economy. The Depression of the 1930s affected Colombia far more profoundly than it affected Venezuela, where petroleum had begun to dominate the economy. Before that, both in colonial times and after independence, Colombia had been consistently ahead of its neighbor both materially and culturally. But in recent decades Venezuela has forged ahead, particularly since the 1950s, when Colombia, heavily dependent on its coffee exports for foreign exchange, began to suffer from a marked and continued decline in coffee prices. To be sure, Venezuela also suffered a setback when the price of petroleum fell in 1958. But this decline was not severe, was of short duration, and in addition was more than counterbalanced by two positive factors: Venezuela's production and export of iron ore, which had started in 1951, more than doubled between 1955 and 1960, making Venezuela the seventh ranking producer in the world; and the restoration

of representative government under President Betancourt cut down on waste and graft, so that the nation got better value for the taxes raised.

By the 1960s, accordingly, although the per capita gross national product of Venezuela was less than a quarter of that of the United States, it was the highest in Latin America and more than twice that of Colombia. And the disparity between the two countries was actually much greater in terms of export earnings. Venezuela's exports in 1964 provided foreign exchange to finance imports equivalent to $244 per capita. Colombia's exports produced only $35 of foreign exchange per person. Although Colombian industry had grown in the 1940s and 1950s, this increasing shortage of foreign exchange began to seriously inhibit further expansion in the 1960s.

EVEN sizable sums supplied by the Alliance for Progress did not solve Colombia's problems. The Alliance was proposed by President John F. Kennedy in March 1961 and was accepted by the nations of Latin America in August of the same year. It committed the United States and the Latin American countries to a joint effort to provide decent living conditions for all the people of the hemisphere by economic development and by a more equitable distribution of the benefits of this progress. To receive aid, each country had to submit a program showing its intention and ability both to increase production and to change its structures so that its most needy citizens would be the primary beneficiaries.

Colombia was the first country to prepare and submit such a program. Anxious to encourage others to follow this example, and also hopeful that Colombia could be made a showcase for the Alliance, the United States responded generously. Using grants and loans from the Alliance to supplement its meager income from exports, Colombia was able to buy the capital goods and raw materials it needed to maintain and expand its industry. However, the social changes that were to have accompanied economic progress were slow to materialize. The Colombian Congress argued endlessly about how to modernize the social structure, its warring factions able to agree only in opposing anyone who threatened to disturb the monopoly of power of the upper class. Colombia's oligarchy not only inhibited changes in the social order but also refused to repatriate the money they had banked or invested abroad as insurance against a revolution at home. Just how much money is involved is hard to determine, but Colombia's President León Valencia estimated it at $900 million in early 1963. This is many times more than the nation's official reserves. Colombia's wealthy are sophisticated and intelligent, but they are immobilized by habits centuries old. "They believe," as one observer has put it, "either that they are powerless to stop the coming social explosion, or that their small improvements will suffice."

Herein lies Colombia's great unsolved problem. It is the cause of endemic violence, the deterrent to foreign investment, and a roadblock in the path of development which even Alliance for Progress funds cannot remove. It is a problem for which Colombians themselves must find the solution. As President Kennedy said in his original appeal to the American nations to join the Alliance: "They and they alone can mobilize their resources, enlist the energies of their people, and modify their social patterns so that all and not just a privileged few share in the fruits of growth."

POLITICAL instability resulting from social conflict thus constitutes the primary obstacle to economic growth in Colombia, whereas Venezuela has surmounted this difficulty, at least for the moment. A similar contrast appears in the Guianas. Both British Guiana and Surinam are anxious to promote industry. However, British Guiana has frightened away new capital because of its failure to solve its racial conflicts and create a stable political situation. Surinam, on the contrary, has licked comparable political problems, and a part of its reward has been the availability of foreign capital which has created a number of new industries. The reservoir of skills and the network of roads and communications created by these industries are serving as a magnet to draw others.

Progress is being made, but at very different rates, in Colombia, Venezuela and at least two of the Guianas. All of these countries have reason to be proud, as they are, of what they have accomplished. But none of them can afford to be complacent because in all a big and growing proportion of the population is living at an unacceptably low level and thereby constitutes a threat to the well-being of the rest of the citizens and to the societies as a whole.

The situation might be thought of as being the opposite of what happened when the region was first colonized by Europeans. The first settlers gradually absorbed the bulk of the Indian inhabitants into their own economy and society, so that they became part of a single culture. The movement was centripetal. Now, however, a centrifugal movement is taking place. The class of people whose poverty and ignorance always cut them off from participation in these cultures has now grown to a point where it is creating a separate society of its own. The 20th Century's population explosion has occurred with the greatest violence among the poor, and the number of impoverished and unskilled has grown to the extent that they now tend to spin off from the society itself and form a subculture that might be likened to a cancerous growth. This subculture depends on the parent society and yet contributes nothing to it. As this mass gets bigger, it becomes more and more costly to maintain even at a subhuman level, and it becomes an ever-greater threat to political stability.

Finding a solution to this problem is the great challenge faced by the people who live in these lands that once lured Europe's dreamers and adventurers because of their imagined stores of gold. The best reason to think that a solution can be found is the fact that these lands do indeed possess great wealth, not in gold and gems but in natural resources, and that the location of this wealth is now known.

THE countries have the arable land to provide a balanced diet for all their people, plus substantial exports and raw materials for manufacture. At least Venezuela and Colombia are rich in coal and oil, and all have great hydroelectric resources. The mineral wealth is almost limitless. And their immense forests constitute an incalculable asset as yet scarcely touched. What is needed is a further reawakening of the same forces that carried the early explorers through dense jungle, over torrid plains, across frozen mountains. It is to be hoped that they will develop the egalitarian pioneer spirit which can properly take advantage of these opportunities.

Lackadaisical soccer players pause beneath the coconut palms of the Place des Palmistes in Cayenne, the capital of French Guiana.

THE SLOW-PACED LIFE *once so prevalent in northern South America* . . .

A fiery young Leftist, Roger Arcaya, speaks out in a debate at the law school of Caracas' Central University, long a hotbed of politica

... is giving way to a new spirit as the people struggle to break free of old patterns,

activity. Arcaya ran in hard-fought 1963 student elections. The issues closely paralleled those that agitate Venezuela's national politics.

insisting on a voice in their governments and a fair share of their nations' wealth

Appendix

HISTORICAL DATES

B.C.

c.10,000 First Indians arrive in Caribbean area and live by hunting big game

A.D.

1498-1501 Christopher Columbus discovers the coastline of Venezuela. Rodrigo de Bastidas explores the coastline of Colombia

1520 First permanent Spanish settlement in Venezuela is established at Cumaná

1525 First permanent settlement in Colombia at Santa Marta

1528 The Spaniards begin to import Negro slaves from Africa

1535-1539 Nikolaus Federmann, Sebastián de Benalcázar and Gonzalo Jiménez de Quesada carry out feats of exploration

1616-1621 Dutch West India Company begins settlement of what is now British Guiana

1630 First settlement in modern Dutch Guiana (Surinam) by British

1643 First major French migration to what is now French Guiana

1667 Treaty of Breda gives Dutch Guiana to the Netherlands in exchange for New Amsterdam (New York)

1799-1815 Dutch Guiana changes hands between Britain and the Netherlands several times

1806 The revolutionary Francisco de Miranda lands at Venezuelan port of Coro, but fails to arouse the people against the Spanish garrison

1810 Wars of Independence begin with revolt in Venezuela

1811 Venezuela declares its independence

1812 Patriots suffer a crushing defeat at Puerto Cabello. Miranda is taken prisoner and shipped to Spain

1813 Simón Bolívar declares a "war to the death" and takes Caracas

1814-1815 New Spanish troops arrive after Napoleon's defeat in Europe. Bolívar flees to Jamaica. Britain is permanently awarded what is now British Guiana by the Congress of Vienna; Netherlands is confirmed in ownership of Surinam

1819 Bolívar crosses the Andes and defeats Spanish troops at Boyacá on August 7, freeing all of Colombia

1821 Spanish army is defeated at Carabobo, thus freeing Venezuela. Congress of Cúcuta unites Colombia and Venezuela as Gran Colombia

1822 Spaniards are defeated at Battle of Pichincha; Ecuador is freed and becomes part of Gran Colombia

1828 Bolívar becomes dictator of Gran Colombia

1830 Venezuela becomes a separate state, withdrawing from Gran Colombia. Bolívar dies on December 17 at Santa Marta on the Caribbean coast

1830-1846 José Antonio Páez rules Venezuela, organizing and developing the country

1834-1838 Slavery is abolished in British Guiana and the country imports indentured laborers, largely Asian Indians, to replace slave labor

1847-1858 Páez goes into exile and José Tadeo Monagas, alternating in office with his brother José Gregorio, gives Venezuela a corrupt and repressive rule

1848 Slavery is abolished in French Guiana

1859-1863 The Federalist War in Venezuela. Páez temporarily resumes power, ruling as dictator from 1861 to 1863. Slavery is abolished in Surinam

1870-1888 Antonio Guzmán Blanco emerges as the new dictator and strongman in Venezuela. Under his rule Venezuela embarks on a period of peace and prosperity

1899-1908 Cipriano Castro marches on Caracas and proclaims himself President. His regime is noted for its extreme corruption

1903 Colombia loses its department of Panama

1908-1935 Juan Vicente Gómez rules Venezuela, crushing all opposing factions

1922-1929 Discovery of major oil supply at Maracaibo in December 1922 begins boom era in Venezuela

1935-1945 Eleazar López Contreras and Isaías Medina Angarita are successively dictators of Venezuela but introduce a number of reforms

1945-1948 A revolt in Venezuela ousts Medina and sets up a provisional junta with Rómulo Betancourt as President. In December 1947 Rómulo Gallegos is elected President in the first popular and democratic election in the nation's history but is overthrown in a military coup d'état 10 months after his inauguration

1946 French Guiana becomes an overseas department of France

1948 Jorge Gaitán, Liberal favorite of the masses in Colombia, is assassinated. Mobs sweep Bogotá for days, looting and burning. Riots spread across the country

1950-1953 Laureano Gómez is President of Colombia. He fails to call Congress into session and all opposition is crushed

1950-1958 Supported by the Army, Marcos Pérez Jiménez rules as a military dictator in Venezuela. He inaugurates a grandiose modernization of Caracas but subjects Venezuela to one of the most rigid and cruel dictatorships that Latin America has ever known

1953-1957 Reign of the dictator Gustavo Rojas Pinilla in Colombia. His Administration is the most savage in the country's history

1954 The Netherlands, Surinam and the Netherlands Antilles declare themselves to be a single kingdom under the Dutch House of Orange

1957 New Colombian Constitution makes the Roman Catholic Church an official part of the state, restores civil government and free elections

1958-1962 Alberto Lleras Camargo, a Liberal, is installed as first President of Colombia's 16-year National Front Government

1958-1963 In Venezuela a coup d'état ousts Pérez Jiménez. A provisional junta organizes democratic elections that bring the Acción Democrática party to power. Rómulo Betancourt becomes President. He undertakes sweeping reforms and the economy improves

1962 Guillermo León Valencia, a Conservative, becomes second President of Colombia's National Front Government

1964 Raúl Leoni becomes President of Venezuela and continues to follow a democratic course

FOR FURTHER READING

CHAPTER 1: THE NORTHERN TIER

Bernstein, Harry, *Venezuela and Colombia*. Prentice-Hall, 1964.

Butland, Gilbert J., *Latin America: A Regional Geography*. Longmans, 1960.

Henao, Jesús María, and Gerardo Arrubla, *History of Colombia*. University of North Carolina Press, 1938.

Jankus, Alfred, and Neil Malloy, *Venezuela: Land of Opportunity*. Pageant Press, 1956.

Schurz, William Lytle, *This New World*. E. P. Dutton, 1954.

Whiteford, Andrew H., *Two Cities of Latin America*. Doubleday, 1964.

Wilgus, A. Curtis, ed., *The Caribbean: British, Dutch, French, United States*. University of Florida Press, 1958. *The Caribbean: Venezuelan Development*. University of Florida Press, 1963.

CHAPTER 2: THE SPANISH CONQUEST

Arciniegas, Germán, *Amerigo and the New World*. Alfred A. Knopf, 1955.

Bourne, Edward Gaylord, *Spain in America, 1450-1580*. Barnes and Noble, 1962.

Kirkpatrick, F. A., *The Spanish Conquistadores*. Meridian Books, 1962.

Morón, Guillermo, *A History of Venezuela*. Roy Publishers, 1963.

Schurz, William Lytle, *Latin America: A Descriptive Survey*. E. P. Dutton, 1963.

CHAPTER 3: WARS OF LIBERATION

Bailey, Helen M., and Abraham P. Nasatir, *Latin America: The Development of Its Civilization*. Prentice-Hall, 1960.

Haring, Clarence Henry, *The Spanish Empire in America*. Harcourt, Brace & World, 1963.

Herring, Hubert, *A History of Latin America*. Alfred A. Knopf, 1961.

Jane, Cecil, *Liberty and Despotism in Spanish America*. Oxford University Press, 1929.

Masur, Gerhard, *Simón Bolívar*. University of New Mexico Press, 1948.

CHAPTER 4: POLITICS AND THE CHURCH

Marsland, William D. and Amy L., *Venezuela through Its History*. Russell & Russell, 1964.

Watters, Mary, *A History of the Church in Venezuela, 1810-1930*. University of North Carolina Press, 1933.

Wilgus, A. Curtis, *South American Dictators*. George Washington Press, 1937.

CHAPTER 5: MODERN ECONOMIC HISTORY

Bailey, Helen M., and Abraham P. Nasatir, *Latin America: The Development of Its Civilization*. Prentice-Hall, 1960.

Bemis, Samuel Flagg, *The Latin American Policy of the U.S.* Harcourt, Brace, 1943.

Bernstein, Harry, *Modern and Contemporary Latin America*. Lippincott, 1952. *Venezuela and Colombia*. Prentice-Hall, 1964.

Christensen, Asher N., *The Evolution of Latin American Government*. Henry Holt and Co., 1951.

Fagg, John Edwin, *Latin America: A General History*. Macmillan, 1963.

Herring, Hubert, *A History of Latin America*. Alfred A. Knopf, 1961.

Holt, Pat M., *Colombia Today and Tomorrow*. Frederick A. Praeger, 1964.

Jane, Cecil, *Liberty and Despotism in Latin America*. Oxford University Press, 1929.

Lavin, John, *A Halo for Gómez*. Pageant Press, 1954.

Lieuwen, Edwin, *Petroleum in Venezuela*. University of California Press, 1954.

Marsland, William D. and Amy L., *Venezuela through Its History*. Russell & Russell, 1964.

Morón, Guillermo, *A History of Venezuela*. Roy Publishers, 1963.

Munro, Dada G., *Intervention and Dollar Diplomacy in the Caribbean: 1900-1921*. Princeton University Press, 1964.

Powelson, John P., *Latin America: Today's Economic and Social Revolution*. McGraw-Hill, 1964.

Rourke, Thomas, *Gómez: Tyrant of the Andes*. Morrow, 1936.

Schurz, William Lytle, *This New World*. E. P. Dutton, 1954.

Tannenbaum, Frank, *Ten Keys to Latin America*. Alfred A. Knopf, 1962.

U.S. Army Area Handbook for Colombia, 2nd ed. U.S. Government Printing Office, 1964.

U.S. Army Area Handbook for Venezuela. U.S. Government Printing Office, 1964.

CHAPTER 6: COLOMBIA

Fluharty, Vernon L., *Dance of the Millions*. University of Pittsburgh Press, 1957.

Holt, Pat M., *Colombia Today and Tomorrow*. Frederick A. Praeger, 1964.

MacEoin, Gary, *Latin America: The Eleventh Hour*. P. J. Kenedy & Sons, 1963.

Martz, John D., *Colombia, A Contemporary Political Survey*. University of North Carolina Press, 1962.

Wickizer, Vernon D., *Coffee, Tea and Cocoa*. Stanford University Press, 1951.

Wilgus, A. Curtis, ed., *The Caribbean: Contemporary Colombia*. University of Florida Press, 1962.

CHAPTER 7: VENEZUELA

Alexander, Robert J., *A Venezuelan Democratic Revolution*. Rutgers University Press, 1964.

Lavin, John, *A Halo for Gómez*. Pageant Press, 1954.

Rourke, Thomas, *Gómez: Tyrant of the Andes*. Morrow, 1936.

Szulc, Tad, *Twilight of the Tyrants*. Henry Holt, 1959.

CHAPTER 8: THE GUIANAS

Bertram, Colin, *In Search of Mermaids*. Crowell, 1964.

James, Preston E., *Latin America*. Odyssey Press, 1959.

Naipaul, V. S., *The Middle Passage*. Macmillan, 1963.

Newman, Peter, *British Guiana: Problems of Cohesion in an Immigrant Society*. Oxford University Press, 1964.

Smith, Raymond T., *British Guiana*. Oxford University Press, 1962.

Swann, Michael, *The Marches of El Dorado*. Dufour, 1958.

Waugh, Evelyn, *Ninety-two Days*. Farrar & Rinehart, 1934.

CHAPTER 9: THE ARTS

Anderson Imbert, Enrique, *Spanish-American Literature: A History*. Wayne State University Press, 1963.

Bailey, Helen M., and Abraham P. Nasatir, *Latin America: The Development of Its Civilization*. Prentice-Hall, 1960.

Eighty Masterpieces from the Gold Museum. Banco de la Republica, Bogotá, 1954.

Hitchcock, Henry Russell, *Latin American Architecture since 1945*. Museum of Modern Art, 1955.

Moholy-Nagy, Sibyl, *Carlos Raul Villanueva and the Architecture of Venezuela*. Frederick A. Praeger, 1964.

Sánchez, George I., *The Development of Education in Venezuela*. U.S. Government Printing Office, 1963.

Smith, Raymond T., *British Guiana*. Oxford University Press, 1962.

Steward, Julian H., ed., *Handbook of South American Indians*, Vol. 2. U.S. Government Printing Office, 1946.

Wilgus, A. Curtis, ed., *The Caribbean: Contemporary Colombia*. University of Florida Press, 1962.

CHAPTER 10: PROGRESS AND PROBLEMS

Bernstein, Harry, *Venezuela and Colombia*. Prentice-Hall, 1964.

Holt, Pat M., *Colombia Today and Tomorrow*. Frederick A. Praeger, 1964.

Martz, John D., *Colombia: A Contemporary Political Survey*. University of North Carolina Press, 1962.

Morón, Guillermo, *A History of Venezuela*. Roy Publishers, 1963.

Wilgus, A. Curtis, ed., *The Caribbean: Contemporary Colombia*. University of Florida Press, 1962. *The Caribbean: Venezuelan Development*. University of Florida Press, 1963.

FAMOUS CULTURAL FIGURES OF COLOMBIA, VENEZUELA AND THE GUIANAS

LITERATURE

Castellanos, Juan de	1522-1607	Spanish-born poet who traveled in New Granada and wrote the history of the conquest in verse. *Elegías de varones ilustres de Indias*
Bello, Andrés	1781-1865	Venezuelan poet and philosopher and first noteworthy writer on Venezuelan themes. *"A la agricultura de la Zona Tórrida"*
Isaacs, Jorge	1837-1895	Colombian novelist. One of Latin America's great fiction writers; combined romantic plot with sentimental descriptions of the Colombian landscape and customs. *María*
Caro, Miguel Antonio	1843-1909	Colombian poet, translator of Vergil and representative of Colombian humanism. *"A la estatua del Libertador"*
Cuervo, Rufino José	1844-1911	Colombian writer who gained international distinction as a linguistic scholar
Pérez Bonalde, Antonio	1846-1892	Venezuelan romantic poet who combined nostalgic themes and realistic regional settings. *"Vuelta a la patria"*
Carrasquilla, Tomás	1858-1940	Colombian novelist and short-story writer whose works are filled with regional characters and regional idiom. *Frutos de mi tierra*
Sanín Cano, Baldomero	1861-1957	Colombian writer. Precise and elegant essayist and critic of his time and culture. *El humanismo y el progreso del hombre*
Silva, José Asunción	1865-1896	One of Colombia's finest lyric poets; often melancholy and elegiac. *"Nocturno"*
Díaz Rodríguez, Manuel	1871-1927	Venezuelan novelist whose favorite theme was the contrasts between the artistic and realistic temperaments. *Sangre patricia*
Valencia, Guillermo	1873-1943	Colombian classical poet who dominated his country's literature in the early 20th Century. *Ritos*
Blanco-Fombona, Rufino	1874-1944	Venezuelan poet and prose writer who sharply portrayed contemporary life. *Cuentos americanos*
Pardo Farelo, Enrique	1883-	Colombian novelist whose pseudonym is Luis Tablanca. *Una derrota sin batalla*
Gallegos, Rómulo	1884-	Venezuela's greatest novelist and most respected man of letters. *Doña Bárbara*
Rivera, José Eustasio	1888-1928	Colombian sonnet writer and novelist of realistic themes and poetic power. *The Vortex*
Parra, Teresa de la	1891-1936	Venezuelan novelist with a charming, gentle and melancholy style. *Las memorias de Mamá Blanca*
Uribe Piedrahita, César	1897-1951	Colombian novelist of regional themes treated in a realistic style. *Mancha de aceite*
Blanco, Andrés Eloy	1897-1955	Venezuelan folkloric poet popular both in the Americas and Spain. *Poda*
Picón-Salas, Mariano	1901-1965	Venezuelan historian, critic and essayist especially known for his cultural histories. *A Cultural History of Spanish America*
Arraiz, Antonio	1903-1962	Venezuelan poet, novelist and short-story writer of social and rural themes. *Puros hombres*
Lichtveld, Lodewijk A. M.	1903-	Surinam diplomat and writer of novels and articles often on regional themes who uses the name of Albert Helman. *De Stille Plantage*
Uslar Pietri, Arturo	1905-	Venezuelan prose writer and playwright whose works began the trend in Venezuela away from naturalism toward a more lyrical realism. *The Red Lances*
Otero Silva, Miguel	1908-	Venezuelan novelist who writes of the decay of society in a vigorous and poetic style. *Fiebre*
Mittelholzer, Edgar Austin	1909-1965	British Guianan novelist whose works are often set in British Guiana and are characterized by lurid fantasy. *Shadows Move Among Them*
Meneses, Guillermo	1911-	Venezuelan novelist and short-story writer of realistic bent who focuses on the psychological depths of his characters. *Tres cuentos venezolanos*
Carter, Martin	1917-	British Guianan Negro poet whose works have contributed to nationalist feelings of Negroes and Indians in British Guiana. *Poems of Resistance*
Seymour, Arthur James	1919-	British Guianan poet, Government official and editor of *Kyk-over-al*, a literary magazine
Medina, José Ramón	1921-	Venezuelan poet who writes intimate lyrical verse. *Círculo poético*

MUSIC

Herrera y Chumacero, Juan	?-1738	Colombian composer of church music and choirmaster of the Cathedral of Bogotá. *Requiem Mass*
Sojo, Padre Pedro Palacios	1739-1799	Father of Venezuelan music. He brought musical scores and instruments from Europe and established an important academy of music in Caracas
Olivares, Juan Manuel	1760-1797	Venezuelan organist and composer of chamber and religious music. *Stabat Mater*
Gallardo, Lino	c.1770-1837	Venezuelan violinist, teacher and composer of secular and patriotic music; one of the most active musicians of his time. *Canción Americana*
Lamas, José Angel	1775-1814	Venezuelan composer of religious music. *Popule Meus*
Landaeta, Juan José	1780-c.1813	Venezuelan composer of religious and patriotic music, including the national anthem, *"Gloria al Bravo Pueblo"*
Larrazábal, Felipe	1816-1873	One of Venezuela's most distinguished 19th Century composers, he was also a pianist, writer, politician and diplomat. *Fantasía brillante sobre "Los Hugonotes"*
Guarín, José Joaquín	1825-1854	Colombian pianist and composer of patriotic works, sacred songs, a mass and works for orchestra. *El Pescador*
Quevedo Arvelo, Julio	1829-1897	Colombian composer of both secular and religious music, he initiated the study of harmony in Colombia

154

Villena, Federico	1835-1899	Venezuelan composer of chamber music and romantic works for orchestra, voice and dance. Comic opera: *Las dos deshonras*
Sindici, Oreste	1837-1904	Colombian composer of national anthem and other patriotic songs
Montero, José Angel	1839-1881	Venezuelan composer of light music and the first opera to be produced in Venezuela: *Virginia*
Ponce de León, José María	1846-1882	Colombian composer who studied in Paris and wrote waltzes, religious music and the first opera to reach the stage in Colombia: *Ester*
Carreño, Teresa	1853-1917	Venezuelan pianist who first drew world's attention to Venezuelan music
Uribe-Holguín, Guillermo	1880-	Colombian conductor, violinist, educator and leading composer. Founder of the Sociedad de Conciertos Sinfónicos del Conservatorio. *Symphonía del Terruño*
Sojo, Vicente Emilio	1887-	Venezuelan teacher and arranger of folk songs. Conductor of Orfeon Lamas, a choral group. Founder and ex-conductor of the Symphony Orchestra of Caracas
Plaza, Juan Bautista	1898-1965	Venezuelan organist and important composer of vocal and instrumental works often using religious themes and traditional style. *Requiem Mass*
Valencia, Antonio María	1902-1952	Colombian pianist, educator and composer of music having a national or regional character. *Sonata Boyacense*
Espinosa, Guillermo	1905-	Colombian conductor. Founded and conducted the National Symphony Orchestra in 1936; later headed the Music Division of the Pan American Union
Estévez, Antonio	1916-	Venezuela's leading contemporary composer. Often uses regional themes. *Cantata Criolla*
Escobar, Luis Antonio	1925-	Colombian composer of works for orchestra, voice, piano, violin and of an indigenous ballet: *Abirana*

PAINTING AND SCULPTURE

Vásquez de Arce y Ceballos, Gregorio	1638-1711	Colombian painter of portraits and religious themes whose works were acclaimed in Europe. He decorated churches in Bogotá
Lovera, Juan	17??-1841	Venezuelan painter who specialized in portraits. His most celebrated work is *5 de Julio*, which portrays the fathers of Venezuelan independence
Tovar y Tovar, Martín	1828-1902	Venezuelan painter. Paris-trained classical portraitist who also did historical scenes. *The Battle of Carabobo*
Garay, Epifanio	1849-1903	Colombian portrait painter with elegant Realistic style
Boggio, Emilio	1857-1920	Venezuelan painter who lived in Paris; Impressionistic tendencies. *Fin de Jornada*
Rojas, Cristóbal	1858-1890	Venezuelan painter who began with historical canvases, later switched to themes of everyday life. Shows influence of Impressionism. *Patio*
Santamaría, Andrés de	1860-1945	Colombian painter who lived mostly in Europe. Influenced by Impressionism. *Still Life with Woman*
Michelena, Arturo	1863-1898	Venezuelan academic Realist painter of diverse themes who used warm colors and experimented with effects of light. *Miranda in the Prison of Carraca*
Salas, Tito	1888-	Venezuelan painter. Commissioned to do walls of National Pantheon and Bolívar's birthplace. *The Miracle*
Reverón, Armando	1889-1954	Venezuelan Expressionist painter whose experiments with light led to his negating all color and using "white light." *Light behind My Arbor*
La Grange, Francis R.	1894-	A convict imprisoned in French Guiana, he has painted prison scenes, native nudes and church frescoes. *Feeding the Animals*
Gómez, Pedro Nel	1899-	Colombian sculptor, architect, engineer and painter of social themes. He painted controversial frescoes for the city hall of Medellín. *Emigración*
Acuña, Luis Alberto	1904-	Colombian painter who began with strongly Realistic works but later experimented with more modern methods, including Surrealism. *The Golden City*
Weidemann, Guillermo	1905-	Colombian painter born in Germany who began as a Figurativist but later switched to Abstract Expressionism. *Collage*
Narváez, Francisco	1908-	Venezuelan sculptor and painter; innovator of modern forms. *Load, Desnudo*
Gómez Jaramillo, Ignacio	1910-	Colombian painter of portraits and social themes. *The Table of the Children*
Ariza, Gonzalo	1912-	Colombian landscape painter showing Japanese influence. *Bogotá*
Poleo, Héctor	1918-	Venezuelan Figurativist painter with Surrealist tendencies. *The Wedding*
Grau, Enrique	1920-	Colombian Figurativist painter with humorous, even frivolous style. *Coqueta 1900*
Negret, Edgar	1920-	Colombian sculptor, considered one of the best in Latin America. *Aparato Mágico*
Obregón, Alejandro	1920-	Colombian painter. Called the father of modern Colombian art, he is a lyrical Geometric Abstractionist utilizing powerful color. *Bull and Condor*
Otero, Alejandro	1921-	Venezuelan painter internationally known for his Abstract paintings and "colorhythms." One of the first practitioners of "Op Art." *Coloritmo No. 66*
Ramírez Villamizar, Eduardo	1923-	Colombian painter of Geometric Abstract works. *Black and White Composition*
Soto, Jesús	1923-	Venezuelan Op artist noted for his painted "line vibrations." *One Blue, Fifteen Blacks*
Gramcko, Elsa	1925-	Venezuelan painter who began as a Geometric Abstractionist but became interested in a more informal style using scraps of metal and sawdust. *Doors*
Valera, Víctor	1927-	Venezuelan Abstractionist painter and sculptor who uses scrap iron, rusty nails and other objects in his works
Manzur, David	1929-	Colombian semi-Abstractionist interested in interspatial forms. *Flora, The Sea*
Jaimes, Humberto	1930-	Venezuelan Abstract painter and stage designer. *Organic*
Botero, Fernando	1932-	Colombian Neofigurativist painter whose works are characterized by bloated monumental forms. *Mona Lisa at 12.*

Credits

The sources for the illustrations in this book appear below. Credits for pictures from left to right are separated by commas, from top to bottom by dashes.

Cover—George Silk
8, 9—Arthur Rickerby
13—Drawings by Matt Greene
17 through 24—Arthur Rickerby
29—Map by Rafael Palacios
32 through 41—Arthur Rickerby
42—Dmitri Kessel
49 through 54—Arthur Rickerby
62 through 69—Arthur Rickerby
72—Map by Rafael Palacios
75, 76, 77—Arthur Rickerby
78, 79—Joseph Fabry except center Arthur Rickerby
80 through 84—Arthur Rickerby
92 through 96—Arthur Rickerby
97—Frank Scherschel—Hernan Diaz, Joseph Fabry
98, 99—Associated Press, United Press International—Joseph Fabry (1)
100, 101—Arthur Rickerby
108—Joseph Scherschel
109—Henry Wallace—Joseph Scherschel—Joseph Fabry

110—Charles Tasnardi
111—Left, Charles Tasnardi—Douglas; right, Charles Moore from Black Star
112 through 116—Arthur Rickerby
123 through 128—Arthur Rickerby
129—Arthur Rickerby except bottom Bob Henriques
130, 131—Bob Henriques except bottom right L. Raatgever
132—Arthur Rickerby
139—Hernan Diaz
140—Hernan Diaz—Frank Scherschel
141—Arthur Rickerby—Joseph Fabry
142—Walter Bennett for TIME, Arthur Rickerby—Frank Lerner for TIME
143—Henry Grossman—Ruth Robertson
144—Arthur Rickerby
149—Arthur Rickerby
150, 151—Joseph Fabry

ACKNOWLEDGMENTS

The editors wish to express their appreciation to A. Curtis Wilgus, Director of Caribbean Conferences, Center for Latin American Studies, University of Florida, who read and commented in detail on the entire text, and to Wanda Rickerby, who provided much of the caption material. Valuable help was also provided by Gilbert Chase, Director, Inter-American Institute for Musical Research, Tulane University; José Gómez-Sicre, Director, Visual Arts Division, Pan American Union; Gregory Rabassa, Associate Professor of Spanish and Portuguese, Columbia University; and Irving Rouse, Professor of Anthropology, Yale University.

The author wishes to express his thanks to Dr. Enrique Soto and Mr. and Mrs. Allen Lowrie, of Bogotá, Colombia; J. Alan Coogan, Dr. Guillermo Morón and Dr. Ramón Yllaramendi, of Caracas, Venezuela; Eduardo Lanz Capriles, of Santo Tomé, Venezuela; John F. McMahon, Harry M. Nassy and Edward R. Wessels, of Paramaribo, Surinam; the Reverend Emmanuel Catty, of Cayenne, French Guiana; and Martin Carter and Paul Persaud, of Georgetown, British Guiana.

Index

Production staff for Time Incorporated
John L. Hallenbeck (Vice President and Director of Production)
Robert E. Foy, Caroline Ferri and Robert E. Fraser
Text photocomposed under the direction of
Albert J. Dunn and Arthur J. Dunn
Four-color scanned separations by
Printing Developments Incorporated, Stamford, Connecticut

✕

Printed by R. R. Donnelley & Sons Company, Crawfordsville, Indiana
and The Safran Printing Company, Detroit, Michigan
Bound by R. R. Donnelley & Sons Company, Crawfordsville, Indiana
Paper by The Mead Corporation, Dayton, Ohio
Cover stock by The Plastic Coating Corporation, Holyoke, Massachusetts

THE CARIBBEAN REPUBLICS
Relief Map

THE CARIBBEAN REPUBLICS
Relief Map

Cities, Towns and Villages

1,000,000 and over   ⊙ 50,000 to 500,000
500,000 to 1,000,000   ∘ 50,000 and below
Rapids

0   50   100   200   300   Miles
0   50   100   200   300   400 Kilometers

NICARAGUA

Huaunta

PROVIDENCIA
(Colombia)

Bluefields

SAN ANDRÉS
(Colombia)

San Juan del Norte

Irazú (Vol.)
11 260

COSTA RICA

San José
Limón

Bocas del
Toro

Gulf of the
Mosquitos

CANAL
ZONE
(U.S.A.)

Colón

Panama

Puerto
Jiménez

David

Gulf of
Chiriqui

COIBA

AZUERO
PENINSULA

Gulf of Darién

PANAMA

Gulf of
Panama

CARIBBEAN   SEA

LESS

PT. GALLINAS

GUAJIRA
PENINSULA

Oranjestad   ARUBA
(Neth.)   CURAÇAO
(Neth.)   BONAIRE
(Neth.)   ROQUES
ISLANDS

Punto Fijo   PARAGUANÁ
PEN.   Willemstad

Ríohacha

Gulf of
Venezuela   Coro   Puerto
Cumarebo

Santa Marta   Tucacas   Maiquetía
Puerto Colombia   Ciénaga   Altagracia   Maracay
Barranquilla   Peak Cristóbal   Villanueva   Cabimas   Puerto Cabello
Colón 18947   Maracaibo   San Felipe
Sabanalarga   Soledad   Carora   Valencia
Cartagena   Calamar   Valledupar   Lake   Barquisimeto   La Victoria
Fundación   Maracaibo   Valera   Acarigua   Los
Machiques   Trujillo   San Carlos

El Carmen   Plato   Encontrados   Bolívar   Guanare   Calabo
Sincelejo   Sincé   Mompós   (La Columna)   Mérida   Barinas   VEN
Lorica   Magangué   El Banco   16 411
Cerete   La Grita   Puerto   Puerto
Monteria   Ocaña   de Nutrias   San Fernando
Cúcuta   San Cristóbal   de Apure
Pamplona   Arauca   R.
Turbo   Puerto   S

Wilches

Ituango   Barrancabermeja   Bucaramanga   Arauca

Yarumal   San Gil   Mt. Ritacuba
Antioquia   Puerto   Socorro   Málaga   18 022
Urrao   Bello   Berrío   Simacota   L
Medellín   Sonsón   Duitama   A
Quibdó   Aguadas   Chiquinquirá   Sogamoso   N
La Dorada   Leiva   Tunja   P
CAPE CORRIENTES   Honda   Zipaquirá   Miraflores   Orocué   San Fernando
Manizales   Chinchiná   Gachetá   Meta   R.   de Atabapo
Pereira   BOGOTÁ   Guaviare   R.
Ambalema   Girardot   Villavicencio   Inirida
Armenia   Ibagué   Tequendama Falls   R.
Buenaventura   Espinal   COLOMBIA   Maroa
Bay of Buenaventura   Buga   Purificación
Chaparral   Calama   Maroa
Cali   Palmira   YAMBI
Puerto   MESA
Tejada   Neiva

MALPELO
(Colombia)   Campoalegre   Vaupés   R.

Popayán   Garzón
Bolívar   San Agustín
Tumaco   La Cruz   Pitalito   Apaporis   R.
Barbacoas   Galeras (Vol.) 13 997   Florencia
Túquerres   Pasto   Içana
Esmeraldas   Tulcán   Ipiales
Otavalo   Ibarra   Puerto   Caquetá   R.   Uaupés
Asís
Equator   Pichincha (Vol.)   Cayambe   Putumayo   R.
15 713
Quito   Cotopaxi (Vol.)   Napo   R.
Bahía de Caráquez   19 344
Manta   Chone   Latacunga   Archidona
Portoviejo   ECUADOR   Tigre   R.
Jipijapa   Ambato   Baños   Japurá
Guaranda   Chimborazo (Vol.)   Pastaza   R.
Babahoyo   20 577   Iça   R.
Guayaquil   Riobamba   São Paulo de
Alausí   Olivença
Gulf of Guayaquil   PERU
Cuenca   Amazon   Solimões
Machala   Azogues   Iquitos   River   Jutai
Sigsig   R.
Tumbes   Santa Rosa   River
Loja   R.

PT. PARIÑAS   Javari   R.
Talara   Marañón   River   Leticia

PACIFIC

OCEAN

ANDES

MOUNTAINS

OCCIDENTAL   MTS.
CENTRAL   MTS.
ORIENTAL   MTS.

PERIJA   MTS.
MÉRIDA   MTS.

Magdalena   River
Cauca   R.
Atrato   R.